2008
ROMAN REPLIES
&
CLSA ADVISORY OPINIONS

REV. JOSEPH J. KOURY, J.C.D.
SR. ROSE MCDERMOTT, S.S.J., J.C.D.
EDITORS, ROMAN REPLIES

MS. SIOBHAN M. VERBEEK, J.C.L.
EDITOR, ADVISORY OPINIONS

REV. MSGR. RONNY E. JENKINS, J.C.D.
MS. JACLYN O'BRIEN MCEACHERN, J.C.L.
DR. LYNDA A. ROBITAILLE, J.C.D.
ASSOCIATE EDITORS, ADVISORY OPINIONS

CANON LAW SOCIETY OF AMERICA

ISBN 1-932208-21-6
ISSN 1543-4230
SAN 237-6296

Table of Contents

ROMAN REPLIES 2008

CLSA ADVISORY OPINIONS

FOREWORD

The Canon Law Society of America publishes annually *Roman Replies and CLSA Advisory Opinions* for canonists and those seeking a clearer understanding of the *praxis legis* of the Catholic Church. The combination of these two services, begun in 1984, continues to serve as useful resources for those involved in the application of canonical discipline.

The compilation of materials for *Roman Replies 2008* is guided by the Reverend Joseph J. Koury, editor, and Sister Rose M. McDermott, S.S.J., associate editor. The collection of entries in this issue, when viewed in conjunction with previous volumes, assists the reader both in understanding recent developments in the law and in identifying current trends in the *praxis* of the Roman Curia.

The selection and assembly of opinions for *CLSA Advisory Opinions 2008* is provided by Ms. Siobhan M. Verbeek, editor and chairperson of the CLSA Advisory Opinions Committee, with the assistance of Monsignor Ronny E. Jenkins, Dr. Lynda A. Robitaille, and Ms. Jaclyn O'Brien McEachern, committee members. The topics addressed in the opinions reflect a variety of canonical issues and demonstrate the scope of canonical expertise and reflection by members of the Society.

Technical support for publication of *Roman Replies and Advisory Opinions* 2008 was provided by Donald+Norwood+Design of Washington, DC.

The *Roman Replies* are collated into successive volumes of the *Canon Law Digest* and periodically *Advisory Opinions* are also collected into larger multi-year volumes, both of which publications are available from the CLSA publications service.

The Canon Law Society of America provides this series as a professional resource. Care should be taken in considering the relative weight of the materials found in this publication. The principles for canonical interpretation (CIC cc. 16-19 and CCEO cc. 1498-1501) serve as guides in considering the contents of this volume.

Sister Sharon A. Euart, R.S.M.
Office of the Executive Coordinator
The Hecker Center, Suite 111
3025 Fourth Street, NE
Washington, DC 20017

Roman Replies

Introductory Note

My sincere thanks to all who sent documents for this current edition of *Roman Replies*, and especially to Rev. Paul Counce, President of CLSA. Some submissions are in need of translation and will be held over until next year's volume.

E-mail has greatly enhanced the speed and availability of relevant responses and documents. Importing texts from different software programs, of course, is a challenge. Some page or typographical errors may have slipped through the process. In addition, please note that several of the documents have been "sanitized" to protect anonymity and confidentiality by changing or removing names, places and dates.

When submitting texts by e-mail for *Roman Replies* it would be helpful to attach a file that admits of electronic copying so that the text can be formatted more easily. This method also assists in maintaining the accuracy of the documentation. Volunteers to translate submitted documents are always needed; they provide a valuable service to our Society.

The most important resource for *Roman Replies* remains the Society's members. Anyone who notices a response or document that would be of interest to canonists can assist the committee greatly by submitting it as soon as possible for consideration. The editor's current e-mail address is jjkoury622@roadrunner.com

Rev. Joseph J Koury, J.C.D.
Editor, *Roman Replies*
St Francis of Assisi Church
Belfast, ME 04915

Sr. Rose McDermott, S.S.J., J.C.D.
Assistant Editor, *Roman Replies*
Dean – Ad Interim
School of Canon Law
Catholic University of America
Washington, DC 20064
mcdermor@cua.edu

Canons 62, 71, and 41

DISPENSATION FROM THE OBLIGATIONS OF THE CLERICAL STATE

This case presents several interesting issues: in 2004, a petition was presented to the Congregation for the Clergy for dispensation from the obligations of the clerical state. In early 2007, the same priest wrote to the Diocesan Bishop rescinding his petition. The Diocesan Bishop forwarded the priest's letter to the Congregation for the Doctrine of the Faith. That same month, the Bishop, while visiting Rome on other business, went to the Congregation for Clergy and was given a copy of the rescript of dispensation: in the intervening time, the Congregation for the Clergy had presented the original petition to the Holy Father who had granted it earlier that same month. In a written response, the Congregation for the Clergy replied to the Bishop that the dispensation must stand and should be communicated to the Petitioner.

What follows is part of the exchange of correspondence. The rescript of dispensation contained the standard provisions and is not reprinted here. The dates are true, since they are pertinent to the case. This is an unofficial English translation prepared by Rev Thomas C. Anslow, C.M., J.C.L., Archdiocese of Los Angeles, who submitted the documentation. He noted the following: the reason for the granting of the original petition is cited: the manner in which the rescript takes effect [at the moment of execution, or notification, with or without the acceptance of the petitioner, Can 62]; that the grant of the petition is not a simply personal matter [sui dumtaxat] but was due to the "radical lack of suitability of the candidate for Holy Orders in the first place;" and that no recourse was available to the petitioner.

May 11, 2007

Dear Bishop,

My name is ____________. I was ordained a priest in the Diocese of ____________ in 1995. After struggles and discernment I left the active ministry, freely and without scandal, and moved to (another state) in 1999. I formally began the process for laicization through the ____________ Diocese about three years ago, after a concentrated time of discernment with Father ____________. As of this time, I still have not received a response from Rome on the matter.

During the period of waiting, I have continued my prayer life and volunteer service, wondering whether I have made the correct choice. I had been engaged to a lady for three years, but this ended about one year ago. I have a stable career, own a condo, teach at my parish and enjoy a fine circle of friends, but despite all this, I am still struggling with the thoughts of returning to active ministry, thinking that I have made a mistake in applying for laicization. In the midst of the trials and struggles during active ministry, my life as a priest was always something that came natural, with purpose and grace. I have not experienced this in my life since leaving active ministry, as if something is not right. I think it is the prudent thing to address this. I hope you can help.

On May 5, 2007, I phoned the nuncio's office and was advised to write this letter to you. Father ___________ agreed. Can you offer me counsel on the matter and if you deem appropriate, intervene in the process. I have always tried to answer God's call and will continue to trust, that however this concludes, it is God's will.

I look forward to hearing from you as soon as possible and speaking with you in further detail.

Yours in Christ
[Signature of petitioner]

Within two weeks, the Bishop responded to the petitioner, and indicated that being "not certain how the Holy See would respond to a case like yours," he would inquire quickly. On that same date, May 23, 2007, the Bishop wrote to the Cardinal Prefect of the Congregation for the Doctrine of the Faith. There followed the bishop's visit to Rome a couple of weeks later, when he was handed the rescript of dispensation.]

A reply from the Congregation for the Clergy is dated July 5, 2007.

Congregation for the Clergy
July 5, 2007

Your Excellency,

This Congregation has received, by reason of competence, your recent letter regarding the Dispensation from the obligations of the Priestly State of ______________, a priest of the Diocese of __________, whose petition was submitted through Your Excellency's kind offices.

The Dispensation in question was granted and mailed to Your Excellency on the 15th May 2007. Your Excellency's letter of May 23 indicates that the individual now wishes to rescind his request. As the Dispensation was granted on the grounds of Article 2 of the Norms currently in effect, that is because of radical lack of suitability of the candidate for Holy Orders in the first place, it is not envisioned that this act of the Supreme Authority of the Pontiff could now be overturned at the simple request of the individual concerned.

Thus, Your Excellency is asked to communicate the Rescript in the normal fashion as per the letter of this Congregation dated 15th May 2007, bearing the above Protocol Number.

I take this opportunity to renew my sentiments of esteem and with every best wish, I remain,

Sincerely yours in Christ,

(signed) + Mauro Piacenza
Titular Archbishop of Vittoriana
Secretary

CANON 223, §2

THE COMMON GOOD AND THE IMPOSITION OF TEMPORARY LIMITS ON THE EXERCISE OF PRIESTLY MINISTRY

The decree presented here, issued by the Congregation for the Clergy, upholds the recourse made by a priest against the decree of his diocesan bishop, which, in effect, permanently suspended him from ministry, citing can. 223, §2 as justification. The recourse was intially presented to the Congregation for the Doctrine of the Faith, which found that the allegations of sexual abuse did not constitute a grave delict because the alleged abuse took place before the priest was a cleric. It was later transferred to the Congregation for the Clergy for a decision.

CONGREGATIO PRO CLERICIS

Decree

Prot. N. ___________

Whereas, the Reverend ___________, a priest of the Diocese of ___________, ordained on ___________ 1990, was accused in 2002 of several instances of sexual abuse with minors that were alleged to have occurred in 198__ or 198__, prior to his becoming a cleric;

whereas, in 2004, after a lengthy treatment of the case in the Diocese of ___________, the acts of the case were transmitted to the Congregation of the Doctrine of the Faith;

whereas, by letter dated ____ March 2005 (Prot. N. ___________) the Congregation for the Doctrine of the Faith determined that the accusations did not constitute a *gravius delictum* because the alleged action was reported to have occurred prior to Father ___________ s having become a cleric;

whereas, the Congregation for the Doctrine of the Faith in the aforesaid letter stated that "if it were not a cause of grave scandal among the faithful and if the priest does not constitute a risk to minors, Your Excellency may wish to give Rev.___________ a pastoral placement within the diocese, taking into consideration canon 223 §2 *CIC*";

whereas, after conducting an investigation, on __May 2006, the Most Reverend ___________, Ordinary of the Diocese of ___________, issued a decree pursuant to can. 223 §2 (the "Decree") imposing a temporary limit on the exercise of the priestly rights of Father ___________ and enjoining him from performing any public ministry "in view of the common good, to minimize the danger of grave scandal, and due to the lack of resolution of certain questions regarding his fitness for presbyteral ministry;"

whereas, the temporary disposition enacted is continually renewed upon its expiration (most recently on ____ December 2007 and having effect until ____ June 2008), it has, in fact, become a permanent exclusion from ministry, albeit by a series of individual dispositions but which, in fact, constitute a continuous administrative act, contrary to the discipline of canon 1342 §2;

whereas there is no indication by the Ordinary of the legitimate means of resolving the outstanding questions regarding the fitness of Father __________ for ministry, thus not affording him the possibility of extricating himself from the alleged incapacity for ministry and thereby again rendering the situation permanent;

whereas, on __June 2006, pursuant to can. 1734, Father __________ requested the revocation of the Decree, a request to which the Ordinary did not respond;

whereas, on __July 2006, Father __________ made recourse against the Decree to the Congregation for the Doctrine of the Faith pursuant to cann. 57 & 1737;

whereas, by letter dated __December 2006 (Prot. N. __________), the Congregation for the Doctrine of the Faith transferred the recourse of Father __________ to the Congregation for the Clergy by reason of its competence in the matter;

whereas, the Congregation for the Clergy in its evaluation of the situation has noted the jurisprudence of the Supreme Tribunal of the Apostolic Signatura (Prot. N. 37937/05CA) which indicates that can. 223 §2 does not grant an Ordinary the authority to remove a priest permanently from public ministry:

Idem Exc.mus Ordinarius dein in recursu ad H.S.T. invocavit can. 223 ad probandum legitimitatem suae decisionis relate ad Rev.dum N.: "canon 223 authorizes an ecclesiastical Superior to restrict the use of certain rights in order to protect the common good" (S. 34). Ad rem haec sedulo notanda sunt: a) can. 223 concludit titulum "De omnium christifidelium obligationibus et iuribus"; b) canones huius tituli (can. 208-223) proveniunt ex schemate Legis Ecclesiae Fundamentalis; c) agitur in illo canone de moderamine illarum obligationum et iurium fundamentalium ad bonum commune tuendum; d) can. 223 tantum principium omnino generale proponit, cuius magis concreta determinatio proprie fit per actus potestatis legislativae, in primis et praeprimis in ceteris normis ipsius CIC; e) quibus Episcopi non possunt derogare, secus actum esset de principio legalitatis et ianua pateret arbitrarietati (cf. V. De Paolis, "Incardinazioni anomale", in L. Navarro, L'Istituto dell'incardinazione, *Milano 2006, 351-377, vide 367-377). Adde quod potestas moderandi exercitium illarum obligationum et iurium haudquaquam aequari potest cum potestate idem exercitium tollendi (cf. F. Daneels, "L'investigazione previa nei casi di abuso sessuale di minori", in J.J. Conn – L. Sabbarese, Iustitia in caritate, Città del Vaticano 2005, 409-506, vide 503).*

Quod si, nihilominus, ex quadam analogia illud principium omnino generale obligationibus et iuribus clericorum applicetur, utcumque praescindi nequit a legibus magis concretis ad rem pertinentibus, quae sua vice utpote normae generales applicandae sunt ratione habita circumstantiarum singularium uniuscuiusque casus concreti. Quibus dictis, iam patet haudquaquam sufficere in re invocationem can. 223 vel remissionem ad art. 9 normarum specialium Statuum Foederatorum Americae Septentrionalis, immo non satis efferri potest periculum arbitrarietis quod ingenua invocatio principiorum ibi propositorum secumfert. Supremo Tribunale Della Segnatura Apostolico *(Exc. mus Episcopus – Congregatio pro Clericis) – 28 aprile 2007 – Prot. n. 37937/05 – Grocholewski, Ponente,* Ius Ecclesiae, *Vol. 19, 2007, 611-626, vide 619-620.*

whereas the Congregation for the Clergy furthermore sought a clarification from the Pontifical Council for Legislative Texts, regarding the application of canon 223 §2 "...da alcuni Ordinari degli Stati Uniti, per 'sospendere, a tempo indeterminatio, o per rimuovere dall'esercizio del sacro ministero' i sacerdoti anche nei casi in cui non hanno commesso un vero e proprio delitto o non vi è stato un processo canonico";

whereas in a response dated 27 June 2008 (N. 11127/2008), the Pontifical Council, having studied the matter with certain experts, stated:

"*...Anzitutto, è necessario ricordare che la prima e fondamentale regola di interpretazione porta a considerare il significato proprio delle parole nel testo e nel contesto (cfr. can. 17). Applicando tale regola all'espressione 'exercitium iurium...moderari', del can. 223, §2 se ne può dedurre il significato ampio di 'governare' nel senso di emanare norme, legiferare...Il Legislatore, quindi, riconosce la capacità dell'Autorità ecclesiastica di disciplinare, mediante leggi, l'esercizio dei dirriti. Non sembra, però, che la* mens *sia stata quella di stabilire con il can. 223 §2 una norma per giustificare un intervento amministrativo del superiore...Quanto ai provvedimenti limitativi dell'esercizio del sacerdozio, come la rimozione dagli uffici pastorali o la revoca di alcune facoltà ministeriali, quali sanzioni amministrative si ritiene che ciò è possibile, però in base ad altre norme, come ad es. il can. 1722, CIC...L'invocazione del can. 223 §2 allo scopo di legittimare gli interventi amministrativi di contenuto di fatto penale risulta, invece, del tutto fuorviante, non solo sotto il profilo tecnico, come un'analisi attenta concluderebbe senza difficoltà, ma anche e soprattuto sotto il profilo della giustizia sostanziale; significherebbe annullare practicamente la stessa legislazione codiciale e collocare il potere amministrativo (penale) al di sopra de quello normativo generale...L'ordinamento canonico ha stabilito che la* *dimissione dello stato clericale esige un processo giudiziale e può essere fatto solo per delitti stabiliti dalla legge universale. Un'invadenza dell'atto amministrativo in questo campo non sembra rispondere all lettera e allo spirito dell'ordinamento canonico..."*

whereas, the Decree (as well as the subsequent similar decrees) cites can. 223 §2 as giving the Ordinary the authority to effectively and continuously remove Father ____________ from the exercise of priestly ministry,

whereas the canonical process involved in the application of this provision was not that envisioned for such a situation by the Code of Canon Law,

therefore, in light of the all the foregoing:

the Congregation hereby decrees that the administrative recourse presented by the Reverend ____________ against the Decree of his Ordinary dated __May 2006 (and subsequent prorogations of same) is upheld because it violates the law both in procedendo and in decernendo.

Article 135 of the General Regulations of the Roman Curia states that an appeal to the Supreme Tribunal of the Apostolic Signatura can be made within thirty (30) days, from the date of the legitimate reception of this Decree.

Given at the Seat of the Congregation for the Clergy ____July 2008

+ Mauro Piacenza
Titular Archbishop of Vittoriana
Secretary

Monsignor J. Anthony McDaid
Department Head

Canon 535

PARISH REGISTERS

Some bishops have inquired about the possibility of allowing microfilming and digitalization of parish records by the Genealogical Society of Utah (Mormons). The Congregation for the Doctrine of the Faith noted the issue and the Congregation for Clergy issued a response which was sent to the Conferences of Bishops. The U.S. Conference of Bishops forwarded this response to all bishops on April 25, 2008.

Congregation for Clergy
Vatican City State
5 April 2008
Protocol N. 20080365

Your Eminence / Your Excellency,

By letter dated 29 January 2008, the Congregation for the Doctrine of the Faith noted an issue raised by some bishops regarding the possibility of allowing the Genealogical Society of Utah (Mormons) to microfilm and digitalize information contained in parish registers.

Sharing the grave reservations expressed by that Congregation, this Dicastery is bringing this matter to the attention of the various Conferences of Bishops. The Congregation requests that the Conference notifies each Diocesan Bishop in order to ensure that such a detrimental practice is not permitted in his territory, due to the confidentiality of the faithful and so as not to cooperate with the erroneous practices of the Church of Jesus Christ of Latter-day Saints.

Trusting that you will understand the motives for this request, I take this opportunity to renew my sentiments of esteem and with every best wish, I remain,

Sincerely yours in Christ,
Claudio Cardinal Hummes
Prefect
(signature) Secretary

Canons 751, 1364

FORMAL ACT OF DEFECTION FROM THE CATHOLIC CHURCH

The following letter clarifies some aspects of an earlier circular letter by the President of the Pontifical Council for Legislative texts concerning the requisites for the formal act of defection that releases a baptized Catholic from the impediment of disparity of cult, the prohibition of mixed marriage, and the obligation of canonical form for the validity of a marriage.

John Huels noted in April 2008 in a list-serv discussion: "The 13 March 2006 circular letter of the Pontifical Council for Legislative Texts made it clear that a formal act of defection had to be received by a competent Catholic ecclesiastical authority. The act of reception by the Catholic authority is a constitutive element of the formal act of defection. It applies retroactively, affecting marriages since the 1983 Code entered into force." The following reply offers a clarification of the requisites.

Reply of Julián Cardinal Herranz
President of the Pontifical Council for Legislative Texts
Communicationes 38 (2006) 185-187.
Vatican City, 24 November 2006

Most Reverend Eminence,

In reference to the circular letter sent from this Pontifical Council, 13 March 2006 (Prot. N. 10279/2006)[1] regarding the formal act of defection from the Catholic Church (*actus formalis defectionis ab Ecclesia catholica*), Your Eminence has asked if the affirmation contained in n. 5 ("It is required, moreover, that the act be manifested by the interested party in written form before the competent authority of the Catholic Church") implies the necessity of presenting oneself in person before the Ordinary or proper pastor or, rather, could it be sufficient for the interested person to send a written petition.

[...] Regarding this matter, it must be taken as a given that the mind of the circular letter of the Holy See is that belonging to or not belonging to the Church is not only a juridical-administrative question of public record but is a delicate theological-canonical question that pertains to the constitutive elements of the life of the Church.

[1] See *Roman Replies 2006*, 31-33; *Roman Replies 2007*, 7.

In fact, only those who knowingly place acts of true apostasy, heresy or schism (cf. cc. 751 and 1364 CIC) are separated from the Church and therefore have the actual intention to break the bonds of communion with the Church, notwithstanding the canonical penal consequences of which they are aware or of which they must be made aware.

It is always desirable that the ecclesiastical authority have personal contact with the member of the faithful who has presented or sent the request or the simple communication of abandonment of the faith. Only he can verify the existence or absence of these free and conscious dispositions of will in the interested party and of the awareness of the relative canonical consequences. In this case, therefore, it is not a matter of an act of regulation of personal facts in the civil order, but an act of great theological-canonical significance placed within the ecclesiastical order, whose autonomy of jurisdiction in this matter is recognized by the State [...].

In the case of one of the faithful who is unwilling to meet in person (which would have permitted the sacred pastor to help the person reflect on the gravity and consequences of the act, and hopefully to motivate a change of the decision), it would be necessary to resort to sending a personal letter in which it is explained with clarity and delicacy that a true act of defection breaks the bonds of communion with the Church which existed from the moment of baptism. It would be necessary to clarify that such a gesture, which qualifies as an act of true apostasy (or heresy or schism, according to the reasons given by the interested party), is so grave that it is considered not only a grave sin but also an ecclesiastical delict, for which is prescribed the most onerous of canonical penalties, namely, excommunication. To help the person understand the gravity of the penalty, it would be suitable to illustrate in a concrete manner the practical effects of excommunication (for example, that without the remission of the penalty one is not able to receive communion or sacramental absolution, that one cannot be a sponsor at baptism or confirmation, that one cannot have ecclesiastical funeral rites, etc). In short, the communication must be a reasoned invitation to consider carefully and eventually change the decision to leave the Catholic Church.

Whenever this invitation, whether orally or in writing, is not accepted - or the letter is received but remains without a response – there will be documentary evidence that the interested party has chosen to place himself formally in a canonical situation of rupture of the ecclesial communion with the corresponding penal consequences, and one could then proceed to make the required annotation. In any case, if it were still possible, it would also be profitable to assist the interested party to understand that, in light of the baptismal character, the ontological bond with the Church remains, and that his return to the Father's house (cf. Luke 15: 11-33) will always be desired.

[...] Hoping to have furnished your Eminence the elements necessary to resolve the doubts in the case before you, I gladly take this occasion to confirm my sentiments of cordial esteem of your Most Reverend Eminence.

Julián Cardinal Herranz
President of the Pontifical Council for Legislative Texts

Canons 849, 869

INVALID BAPTISM FORMULA

On February 22, 2008, the United States Conference of Catholic Bishops circulated a document entitled "Responsa ad proposita dubia" with an Explanatory Article, sent by William Cardinal Levada, Prefect of the Congregation for the Doctrine of the Faith, to the Presidents of the Episcopal Conferences, regarding the formula of words used at Baptism. Cardinal Levada's letter is dated February 6, 2008, with the note that the "Responsa" would be published on March 1, 2008 in L'Osservatore Romano, *until which time it remained strictly confidential.*

The text of the letter is addressed to the Presidents of the Episcopal Conferences. The "Responsa" is "Enclosure 1" and the "Explanatory Article," written by Msgr. Antonio Miralles, is "Enclosure 2."

Congregation for the Doctrine of the Faith
February 6, 2008

Your Eminence/Your Excellency,

In response to a number of inquiries, this Congregation has conducted a study into the validity of various formulas which use so-called "inclusive language" for the conferral of the sacrament of Baptism.

Having completed the study, this Dicastery is now in a position to publish its response to these queries in the form of a *Responsa ad proposita dubita* (cf. enclosure 1) together with an explanatory article (cf. enclosure 2).

The *Responsa* will be published on March 1, 2008 in *L'Osservatore Romano*, until which time it remains strictly confidential.

This Dicastery would be grateful if you would forward the enclosed documentation to all the Bishops of the Conference of which you are President in good time, so that they will be informed about the *Responsa* prior to its publication.

With many thanks for your cooperation in this matter and wishing you every blessing, I am,

Yours sincerely in Christ,
William Cardinal Levada, prefect

ENCLOSURE 1: RESPONSA

Responses to Questions Proposed on the Validity of Baptism Conferred With the Formulas

"I baptize you in the name of the Creator, and of the Redeemer, and of the Sanctifiers"

and

"I baptize you in the name of the Creator, and of the Liberator, and of the Sustainers"

QUESTIONS

FIRST QUESTION: Whether the Baptism conferred with the formulas *"I baptize you in the name of the Creator, and of the Redeemer, and of the Sanctifiers"* and *"I baptize you in the name of the Creator, and of the Liberator, and of the Sustainers"* is valid?

SECOND QUESTION: Whether the persons baptized with those formulas have to be baptized *in forma absoluta*?

RESPONSES

TO THE FIRST QUESTION: Negative.

TO THE SECOND QUESTION: Affirmative.

The Supreme Pontiff Benedict XVI, at the Audience granted to the undersigned Cardinal Prefect of the Congregation for the Doctrine of the faith, approved these Responses, adopted in the Ordinary Session of the Congregation, and ordered their publication.

Rome, from the Offices of the Congregation for the Doctrine of the Faith, February 1, 2008.

William Cardinal Levada *Prefect*

Angelo *AMATO, S.D.B Secretary*

ENCLOSURE 2: EXPLANATORY ARTICLE

"A New Response of the Congregation for the Doctrine of the Faith on the Validity of Baptism" by Msgr Antonio Miralles

Baptism, the "water of rebirth and renewal by the Holy Spirit" (Tit 3:5), constitutes one of the most precious gifts with which the Lord Jesus has enriched his Church. Indeed, by means of Baptism "we are freed from sin and reborn as sons of God; we become members of Christ, are incorporated into the Church and made sharers in her mission."[2] It is understandable, therefore, that Christians in every age have concerned themselves with its correct celebration, in order that it might correspond exactly to the original will of Christ himself. Doubts were not minimized when they arose, but on the contrary Christians sought to guarantee true Baptism. Of course, the Church's Magisterium has a decisive role in this

[2] *Catechism of the Catholic Church*, 1213

work of clarification. Interventions of the Holy Office and the Congregation for the Doctrine of the Faith in recent centuries have reflected this care for the validity of Baptism; in the past two decades, there have been three.[3]

The present *Response* concerns a question about the validity of Baptism conferred with the Catholic Church with two specific formulas in the English language. This element is significant, because it indicates that this is not simply a hypothetical question, but rather relates to events that have taken place in some English-speaking countries. Obviously, the problem does not relate to the fact that the words are in the English language, but to the formula itself, which could be expressed in any language.

The importance of this problem cannot be minimized, since it is a matter of people's salvation, which, according to the Lord himself, requires Baptism: "Amen, amen, I say to you, no one can enter the kingdom of God without being born of water and the spirit" (*Jn 3:5*). From this comes the mission to baptize which Jesus entrusted to the disciples: "Go into the whole world and proclaim the Gospel to every creature. Whoever believes and is baptized will be saved, whoever does not believe will be condemned" (*Mt 16:15-16*). Therefore, the Church cannot tolerate the use of formulas which invalidate the conferral of true Baptism. It would furthermore be irresponsible to minimize this danger by comforting oneself with the thought that God is able to remedy all human failures. Instead, we are called to carry out well that which God has entrusted to our responsibility.

Baptism conferred in the name of the Father, the Son and the Holy Spirit conforms to the command of the Lord found at the end of Matthew's Gospel: "Go therefore and make disciples of all nations, baptizing them in the name of the Father and of the Son and of the Holy Spirit" (*Mt 28:19*). Therefore, any Baptism is invalid when it does not contain the invocation of the Most Holy Trinity, with the distinct expression of the three Persons with their respective names. Throughout the ages, the Magisterium of the Church has repeatedly taught that Christian Baptism is administered in the name of the Father and of the Son and of the Holy Spirit. There is no need here to compile a complete list of the relevant magisterial documents; it may suffice to cite some of the more notable one:

[3] *Responsum ad propositum dubium de validitate baptismatis apud communitatem "The Church of Jesus Christ of Latter-day Saints," 5 June 2001: AAS 93 (2001) 476; Notificatio de validitate baptismatis apud "The New Church" confessionem collate, 20 November 1992: AAS 85 (1993) 179; Notificatio de validitate baptismatis apud "Christian Community" Rudolfi Steiner confessionem, 9 March 1991: AAS 83 (1991) 422.*

the *Tomus Damasi* (382),[4] the decretals *Desiderabillem mihi* of Pope Saint Gregory II (726),[5] and *Sacris liminibus* of Pope Saint Zacharian (748),[6] the chapter *De fide catholica* of the Fourth Lateran Council (1215),[7] the constitution *Fidei catholicae* of the Council of Vienne (1312),[8] the bull *Exsultate Deo* of the Council of Florence (1430), [9] the decree *De sacramentis* of the Council of Trent (1547).[10] The liturgical documents on the Rite of Baptism do not offer alternatives to the terms Father, Son and Holy Spirit.

Sacramental formulas are to be examined as expressions of the faith of the Church. They are words of faith, from which they derive their efficacy, as Saint Augustine clearly shows in regard to the baptismal formula.[11] Saint Thomas Aquinas, commenting on this passage from Saint Augustine, states that in the sacraments the words are efficacious not simply because they are pronounced, but because they express that which is the object of faith.[12] This is what is con-

4 … "for we are baptized solely in the Father and the Son and the Holy Spirit" (H. Denzinger – A Schonmetzer, *Enchiridion Symbolorum definitionum et declarationum de rebus fidei et morum*, [=DS], 176.

5 "you should hold to the ancient practice of the Church: that whoever has been baptized in the name of the Father and of the Son and of the Holy Spirit must in no case be rebaptized" (DS 580).

6 "If someone was immersed in the baptismal font without the invocation of the Trinity, he has not been perfected, unless he will have been baptized in the name of the Father and of the Son and of the Holy Spirit" (DS 589).

7 "But the sacrament of Baptism (which is a consecration in water at the invocation of God and the indivisible Trinity, that is, of the Father and of the Son and of the Holy Spirit) is profitable unto salvation for children as well as adults, by whomsoever it is correctly conferred according to the form established by the Church {DS 802).

8 "One Baptism, which regenerates all who are baptized in Christ must be faithfully confessed by all just as "one God and one faith" (*Eph* 4:5). We believe that baptism, celebrated with water in the name of the Father and of the Son and of the Holy Spirit, is the perfect remedy for salvation for adults and children in common" (DS 903).

9 "… the form is: *I baptize you in the name of the Father and of the Son and of the Holy Spirit*" (DS 1314).

10 "If anyone says that the Baptism which is conferred also by heretics in the name of the Father and of the Son and of the Holy Spirit with the intention of doing what the Church does, is not true Baptism, let him be anathema" (DS 1617).

11 "From where does the water have such power, that it touches the body and cleanses the heart, except by the word which is acting – not because it is spoken, but because it is believed? For also in the word itself, the sound that passes away is one thing, the power that remains is something else" (*in Iohannis Evangelium*, tr. 80, 3: CCL 36, p. 529).

12 "As Augustine says in his *Commentary on John's Gospel*, the word is operative in the sacraments 'not because it is spoken,' that is not according to the exterior sound of the voice, but 'because it is believed,' according to the meaning of the words which is held by faith" (*Summa theologiae*, III, q. 60, a. 7, ad 1).

tained in the pronouncements of the Magisterium cited above. The baptismal formula must adequately express the Trinitarian faith: approximate formulas cannot do this.

The variants to the baptismal formula treated in the *Response* employ terms for the Divine Persons which are different from those found in the Bible. Such formulas result from certain feminist ideas about God, in order to avoid saying Father and Son, which are considered sexist. But substituting other names for Father and Son undermines our faith in the Trinity.

In order to express in synthesis the Trinitarian faith, we can turn to the Athanasian Creed, which is cited in the *Catechism of the Catholic Church*: "Now this is the Catholic faith: We worship one God in the Trinity and the Trinity in unity, without either confusing the Persons or dividing the substance; for the person of the Father is one, the Son's another, the Holy Spirit's another; but the Godhead of the Father, Son and Holy Spirit is one, their glory equal, their majesty coeternal."[13] The names of the three Divine Persons are those by which they are repeatedly designated in the New Testament and in the Tradition of the Church. They are relative names, that is to say, they designate the Persons as they relate to each other with regard to origin, by which they are distinguished. Indeed, "because it does not divide the divine unity, the real distinction of the Persons from one another resides solely in the relationships which relate them to one another."[14] God "is eternally Father in relation to his only Son who is eternally Son only in relation to his Father,"[15] and the "Holy Spirit is ... revealed as another divine Persons" in relation to Jesus and to the Father."[16]

The names *Creator*, *Redeemer* and *Sanctifier* or *Creator*, *Li*berator and *Sustainer* can be attributed to the divine Persons by appropriation, according to the logic that what is common to the three Persons is attributed to one of them, inasmuch as it has a certain likeness to what is proper to the Persons.[17] For example, being Creator is attributed to the Father because, in the act of creating, the divine power is shown in the highest way as the principle of the being of creatures. This power has a certain likeness to what is proper to the Father in the inner-trinitarian life, that is, being the unoriginated principle of the other Persons.[18]

[13] DS 75, cited in the *Catechism of the Catholic Church*, 266.
[14] *Catechism of the Catholic Church*, 255.
[15] *Catechism of the Catholic Church*, 240.
[16] *Catechism of the Catholic Church*, 243.
[17] Cf. Saint Thomas Aquinas, *Summa theologicae*, I, q. 39, a. 7.
[18] Cf. Saint Thomas Aquinas, *Summa theologicae*, I, qq. 39, a. 8 et 45, a. 6, ad 2-3.

But "creation is the common work of the Holy Trinity."[19] Pope Leo XIII taught in general terms, "The Church is accustomed most fittingly to attribute to the Father those works in which power excels, to the Son those in which wisdom excels, and to the Holy Spirit those in which love excels. Not that all perfections and external operations of the Trinity are not common to the divine Persons; indeed, 'the operations of the Trinity are indivisible, even as the essence of the Trinity is indivisible.'[20] "[21]

The Trinitarian faith is not adequately expressed when the three divine Persons are designated by names common to the three, while attributing by appropriation each individual name to a Person. And this is what happens in the formulas considered by the *Response*. All three divine Persons are Creator, Sanctifier, Liberator and Sustainer. "The whole divine economy is the common work of the three divine Persons. For as the Trinity has only one and the same nature, so too does it have one and the same operation."[22] Redemption is also the work of the entire Trinity as its first cause even though the name Redeemer is proper to Christ as man because, in his humanity, he suffered and died on the Cross.[23]

Trinitarian faith calls for careful precision in language. If the substitution of the names of the divine Persons in the baptismal formula by other names that are proper to each of them (Parent, Child and Issue from both) had given rise to such serious doubt among the theologians that Thomas Aquinas considered it invalid,[24] then there is all the more reasons to hold that what is conferred with the formulas considered in the questions presented to the Congregation for the Doctrine of the Faith is not true Baptism.

Therefore, a person who performs a baptism with one of these invalid formulas defrauds the recipient of this action. In the case of a child, he also defrauds those who present the child for Baptism, because they are expecting a true Baptism. This is a grave injustice which must be remedied without delay, not postponed indefinitely based on the efficacy of the desire for Baptism. The gift of the sacramental character of Baptism must be guaranteed as soon as possible: "Baptism seals the Christian with the indelible spiritual mark (character) of his

[19] *Catechism of the Catholic Church*, 292.

[20] Saint Augustine, *De Trinitate*, I 4: PL 42, 824.

[21] Encyclical Letter, *Divinum illud munus*, 9 May 1897: DS 3326.

[22] *Catechism of the Catholic Church*, 258.

[23] Cf. Saint Thomas Aquinas, *Summa theologicae*, III, q. 48, a.5.

[24] Cf. Saint Thomas Aquinas, *Scriptum super Sententiis*, IV, d. 3, q. 1, a. 2, s. 2, ad 5; *Summa theologicae*, III, q. 66, a. 5, arg. 7 et ad 7.

belonging to Christ ... Incorporated into the Church by Baptism, the faithful have received the sacramental character that consecrates them for Christian religious worship."[25]

The ecumenical importance of guaranteeing true Baptism is clearer now than ever before. We call ourselves Christians in virtue of our common Baptism. With regard to the numerous persons who belong to Churches or Ecclesial communities not in full communion with the Catholic Church, even if thee are deficiencies with regard to faith, the other sacraments and Church governance, "Baptism constitutes the sacramental bond of unity, which exists among all those who by mean of it have been regenerated." [26] If a Community relinquishes true Baptism, it takes a great step backwards on the path of ecumenism, by distancing itself tremendously from the desired goal of full communion that Christ himself desires.[27] All of us Christians are called to remain solidly faithful to the unity expressed so well in the Letter to the Ephesians: there is "one Lord, one faith, one Baptism, one God and Father of all, who is above all and through all and in all" (*Eph* 4:5-6). Strengthened by this intervention of the Congregation for the Doctrine of the Faith, the Church's pastors must also be vigilant regarding other possible invalid baptismal formulas.

[25] *Catechism of the Catholic Church*, 1272-1273.

[26] Second Vatican Council, Decree *Unitatis redintegratio*, 22/2.

[27] Cf. Second Vatican Council, Decree *Unitatis redintegratio*, 4/1.

Canons 1156 -1157

PROCEDURES TO BE FOLLOWED IN DECLARATIONS OF INVALID CONVALIDATION

A large number of Tribunals has reported that the Apostolic Signatura has over the past year or so been cautioning Tribunals about the way in which such cases should be adjudicated.

When the officers of the CLSA visited the Rota in Rome in May 2008, they asked for and were provided with a Definitive Sentence for publication which is of considerable interest. In his letter forwarding the sentence, Rev Paul Counce noted: "It is the decision which flowed from a concession of the favor of new hearing by the Signatura. The 2005 decree of the latter was published in Periodica, *and fundamentally objected to the way in which the Rota and subordinate Tribunals had been handling cases on the grounds of Defective Convalidation. The publication of the decree was accompanied by voluminous commentary thereon (80+ pages) by now-Cardinal Navarrete."*

Father Augustine Mendonça, who is presenting a seminar on this topic at the 2008 CLSA convention, has prepared the following translation and sanitized the specific references to render them anonymous. The Latin text of the In Iure section is included immediately after the English translation. At the end of the Sentence we are also printing a sample of the letters sent from the Signatura to a number of Bishops.

Defective Convalidation
Decision *coram* Yaacoub, 19 July 2007[28]

1 — The Facts

1. Brian Cabrini, the petitioner in the case, and Juliana Brown, the respondent, both Catholics, who had received accurate formation in the true faith, attempted marriage before a civil magistrate, that is to say, before a "Justice of the Peace."

Three months later, after completing also the canonical investigation including even the pastoral preparation of the parties to properly and fruitfully contract marriage, the parties finally manifested their conjugal consent in the canonical rite before the Associate Pastor of their parish of St. Helena, which was situated

[28] Decision *c.* Yaacoub, 19 July 2007 (Antioch). English translation by Rev. Augustine Mendonça, JCD. Translated and published with permission of the Dean of the Roman Rota.

within the territory of the diocese of Antioch. The officiating priest was endowed with the necessary faculties. And one cannot deny that the parties at the time were deeply in sincere and unconditional love for each other.

2. Already during their studies at the college, which was situated in the city of Antioch, the two young people developed first a friendly and then a love relationship. The parties were so physically attracted toward each other that they indulged in sexual relationship which resulted in the woman's pregnancy. Following this they entered into a civil marriage. Then, in order not to remain in a sinful state, they sought a canonical marriage.

The marriage was gifted with several children. The partnership of conjugal union lasted a long time, however not without problems, dissensions, arguments and marital difficulties between the parties, and with the passage of time these problems became worse, which finally led to their definitive separation. Seven years later the petitioner obtained a civil divorce.

3. Because there was no possibility of reconciliation between the parties, the petitioner presented the introductory *libellus* before the tribunal of Antioch, competent by reason of the place of marriage, by which he sought a declaration of nullity of his marriage with the respondent due to *consensual incapacity on his own part*.

In order to avoid any suspicion because of the condition of the petitioner, by Decree of the Supreme Tribunal of the Apostolic Signatura, the case was transferred to the tribunal of Smyrna to be judged in the first grade of jurisdiction, where a judicial college was constituted and the *libellus* was admitted. Then the doubt was determined by decree according to the formula: "*Whether the marriage of Brian Cabrini and Juliana Brown was null on the ground of lack of discretion of judgment on the part of the Petitioner or Defective convalidation on the part of the Petitioner or defective convalidation on the part of the Respondent.*"

When the instruction of the case was completed through a judicial examination of the parties and of twelve witnesses who were introduced, as well as through the acquisition of pertinent documents, the acts were published. Then, after obtaining the observations both of the defender of the bond and of the parties as well as of the advocates of the parties, the first instance tribunal that was approached pronounced a decision partly in favor of the petitioner's wishes, that is, "*There is no proof of nullity of marriage in the case either due to defect of discretion of judgment in the petitioner or due to defect of convalidation on his part. On the other hand, there is proof of nullity of marriage due to defect of convalidation of consent on the respondent's part.*"

4. After the sentence was published and the parties were notified of it, the respondent raised a complaint of nullity against this sentence before the first instance tribunal of Smyrna. The same tribunal by decree upheld the validity of the sentence of first instance.

Then the woman herself appealed to Our Apostolic Tribunal against the affirmative sentence of first instance, that is, against the ground of invalid convalidation of consent on the part of the woman respondent. After fulfilling the requirements of law, the Fathers of the *Turnus*, and having considered the *votum* of the defender of the bond, admitted the case to an ordinary examination.

The *Turnus* by decree determined the doubt on the only ground that had received the affirmative decision according to the following formula: "*Whether there is proof of nullity of marriage in the case due to defect of the new act of the will on the part of the woman respondent in convalidating the marriage (can. 1156, §2; 1157 CIC).*

After the new *Ponens* was appointed in the place of the preceding one, a supplementary instruction of the case was carried out. After the acts were published and the observations of the defender of the bond and briefs of the advocates of the parties were exchanged, the Rotal *Turnus* issued an affirmative decision, that is, "*There is proof of nullity of marriage in the case due to a defect of convalidation of consent on the part of the woman respondent*," thus fully confirming the appealed decision of Smyrna.

5. The defender of the bond was not satisfied with this. He presented a reasoned recourse to obtain a new proposition of the case. After the briefs of the advocates of the parties as well as of the defender of the bond were presented, the *Rotal Turnus by decree rejected the requested new proposition of the case.*

However, the defender himself placed recourse against the said Rotal decree before the Supreme Tribunal of the Apostolic Signatura to obtain a new proposal of the case. Therefore, through the letter of the Dean the acts were transmitted to the Supreme Tribunal of the Apostolic Signatura, which, after carefully weighing everything required by law, by decree stated: "*A new proposition of the cause in the case must be granted and is in fact granted.*"

By order of the Dean addressed to the *Ponens*, after this decree was communicated to the defender of the bond and to the advocates, a *Turnus* was constituted by the decree of the same Dean to adjudicate the cause anew.

The doubt was determined by decree under the following formula: "*Whether there is proof of nullity of marriage in the case on the ground of defect of convalidation of matrimonial consent on the part of the woman respondent.*" And after having received the written defenses of the parties, similarly having obtained the observations of the depute defender of the bond, and after these have been reviewed by the principal defender of the bond, we ought to respond to this doubt.

2 — The Law

DEFECTIVE CONVALIDATION

6. The consent of the parties legitimately manifested between persons qualified by law, makes marriage; no human power is able to supply it. This principle must be upheld in light of the prescript of both the old Code of Canon Law (c. 1081, §1) and the present Code (c. 1057, §1). Paul VI said the following concerning matrimonial consent: "In virtue of this well-known principle, a marriage exists at the moment when the spouses express a juridically valid matrimonial consent. ... Consequently, once the consent has produced its juridical effect, it automatically becomes irrevocable and lacks power to destroy what it created" (Paul VI, Allocution to the Roman Rota, 9 February 1976, in *AAS*, 68 [1976], p. 206).

If one of those who marry is a baptized Catholic, the conjugal consent must be presented according to the canonical form (c. 1099 *CIC/17*; c. 1117 *CIC/83*).

7. A merely apparent and invalid marriage can be verified when, according to canon law, the juridic effect of a marriage that was celebrated can be deficient in three ways, namely when there was a diriment impediment (c. 1113 *CIC/17*; 1156 *CIC/83*), or a true internal consent was deficient in either party (c. 1136 *CIC/17*; c. 1156 *CIC/83*), or the canonical form that was used was defective (c. 1137 *CIC/17*; c. 1160 *CIC/83*).

Because in these cases the marriage is invalid and the spouses continue to live together, canon law provides two ways in which to regularize it, namely either through simple convalidation or through radical sanation.

Simple convalidation is applied if the marriage was invalid either because of a diriment impediment or because of defect of consent. And in the case of an impediment the marriage is convalidated by the cessation of or by a dispensation from the impediment together with a renewal of consent on the part of the one conscious of the impediment. In case of a defect of consent, "if the party who did not consent now consents, provided that the consent given by the other party perseveres" (cf. c. 1136 *CIC/17*; c. 1159 *CIC/83*). However, if the defect of consent was also external and could be proven, it is necessary that the consent is given in canonical form (c. 1136, §3 *CIC/17*; c. 1159, §3 *CIC/83*). Likewise, a marriage that is invalid because of defective canonical form, to be valid, it must be contracted in canonical form (cf. c. 1137 *CIC/17*; c. 1160 *CIC/83*).

For a valid simple convalidation, ecclesiastical law requires the renewal of consent, that is, for a true matrimonial bond to arise at the moment of convalidation, "a new act of the will concerning marriage which is known to have been null from the beginning" (c. 1134 *CIC/17*) is necessary. A similar determination is provided in c. 1156 of *CIC/83*.

"Ecclesiastical law requires this renewal for the validity of [the convalidation] even if each party gave consent at the beginning and did not revoke it afterwards" (c. 1333, §2 *CIC/17*; c. 1156, §2 *CIC/83*).

8. However, the question whether the institute of convalidation, understood in the strict sense, can be applied to a marriage where there was total lack of the required canonical form, is disputed.

For, if a Catholic party attempts marriage before a civil authority or a minister of another religion (i.e., without dispensation from the canonical form), such a celebration obviously lacks all elements of the canonical form and it is rightly described as an "inexistent marriage," because it does not have any semblance or figure of marriage.

In the case of a civil marriage of those baptized in the Catholic Church or received into it, if, according to the present law, they have not defected from it by a formal act (c. 1117 *CIC/83*), the marriage is certainly null and it is clear that the nullity depends on the defect of due form; but many experts in canon law prefer rather to speak of an inexistent marriage in the case.

As evidenced by the writings of many authors truly expert in canonical matters, the long canonical tradition holds that, in the strict sense, the expression and the institute of "convalidation" cannot in any way be applied to the marriage of a Catholic party celebrated simply civilly and without observing the canonical form. For, the fundamental requisite and limit for the application of convalidation is always an invalid marriage. The marriage of a Catholic party celebrated only civilly, without dispensation from the canonical form, does not meet the precise definition of an invalid marriage because such a civil marriage does not in any way have the semblance or figure of a true marriage.

"Convalidation of marriage is an act whereby that which had only the appearance of a true marriage becomes real, when what was deficient in it before is now supplied" (T. Vlaming, *Praelectiones iuris canonici*, vol. II, p. 349, n. 760). And so, "Simple convalidation of marriage is an act by which an invalid marriage is rendered valid with the renewal of consent" (P. Gasparri, *Tractatus canonicus de matrimonio*, ed. nova ad mentem *Codicis I.C.*, vol. II, In Civitate Vaticana, Typis polyglottis Vaticanis, 1932, p. 253, n. 1189).

"Convalidation of marriage is an act by which a marriage that was celebrated before according to the prescribed form, but invalid because of some defect of the form itself or of consent, or because of a diriment impediment, is sanated and becomes valid. Therefore, there is no convalidation properly so-called unless there is at least a semblance of a true marriage. Nor can one speak of convalidation if it is a matter of a marriage that was validly but only illicitly celebrated" (M. Conte a Coronata, *Institutiones iuris canonici ad usum utriusque cleri et scholarum. De sacramentis tractatus canonicus*, tomus III, *De matrimonio et de sacramentalibus*, Romae, Marietti, 1957, p. 933).

In the same way, Wernz–Vidal wrote: "Convalidation of a marriage is an act whereby a marriage previously celebrated invalidly, but with the appearance of legitimacy and form, is so restored that it acquires its validity" (F.X. Wernz – P. Vidal, *Ius canonicum*, tomus V, *Ius matrimoniale*, 3a ed., Romae, Apud Aedes Universitatis Gregorianae, 1946, p. 852, n. 652).

According to A.C. Jemolo, "... today it is certain that a civil marriage of Catholics is, as far as the Church is concerned, inexistent as a marriage, and not just a null marriage because of a defect of form; therefore, one cannot speak of a simple convalidation. Between Catholics, the canon is applicable only in cases of a marriage null because it was contracted before a bishop or a parish priest who celebrated outside their territory, or who lacked one of the conditions indicated in c. 1095, §1, or before a priest who had no permission or with an invalid permission or with a permission subject to a condition that had not been verified, or without the presence of witnesses" (A.C. Jemolo, *Il matrimonio nel diritto canonico*, Milano, Francesco Varaldi, 1941, p. 307, n. 165).

"For Jemolo, therefore, if we understand his mind correctly, in the case of a merely civil marriage of Catholics, convalidation not only does not happen, nor can it happen because, one cannot speak, in the case, of a true first celebration of marriage. In other words, the canon must be applied where the form was deficient, and not where it was totally lacking" (decision *c.* Funghini, 30 June 1988, in *RRT Dec.*, 80 [1988], pp. 440-441, n. 2).

Also F. Galtieri, versed in oriental language, states: "One convalidates an invalid marriage; the absence of marriage is not a null marriage. Therefore, one cannot speak of convalidation when it is a matter of regularizing a situation of two persons who have been living in a concubinage" (F. Galtier, *Le mariage: discipline orientale et discipline occidentale*, [Beyrouth, Université St. Joseph, Faculté de Théologie], 1950, p. 357).

In light of these views, it seems very difficult to speak in absolute terms of a civil marriage as inexistent as far as the Church is concerned, because the same marriage, provided that it was entered into with marital affection and the consent given under the appearance and external figure of a lawful marriage perseveres, can be radically sanated according to c. 1139, §1 *CIC/17* (c. 1162, §1 *CIC/83*).

According to the mind of the cited canon, therefore, we must say that we are dealing more correctly with a juridically inefficacious marriage.

In fact, one can admit without difficulty that the contractants, even if they are baptized in the Catholic Church or converted to it from heresy or schism, when marrying before the civil authority really want to become true spouses in the internal and external forum. Their consent, however, which might have been naturally sufficient, is juridically inefficacious in the absence of the necessary canonical form, by which they are bound under the penalty of nullity of the marriage in virtue of c. 1099, 1° (cf. c. 1117 *CIC/83*).

9. The mind of the Legislator, therefore, seems to exclude simple convalidation for civil marriages, because the canonical form is totally absent in them.

For, in the 1980 schema drafted by the Pontifical Commission for the Revision of the Code of Canon Law, it was declared in c. 1014, which corresponds to c. 1061 of the Code presently in force: "§4. Also a civilly contracted marriage, which is invalid due to defect of canonical form, is understood as an invalid marriage." But later this paragraph was omitted, and the Secretary responded to the omission as follows: "As to §4: It is suppressed, because it is really possible to lead to erroneous conclusions, nor does its omission impede radical sanation, which can be granted even if the marriage is null" (*Communicationes*, 15 [1983], p. 224).

Indeed, the present Code on radical sanation speaks of the form that was not observed, "[dispensation] from canonical form, if it was not observed" (c. 1161, §1), because in simple convalidation there is a figure of "defect of form" (cf. c. 1160 *CIC/83*). Thus it brings out the distinction between the absence of canonical form and the defect of canonical form.

Therefore, even in the present Code, the marriage of a Catholic party celebrated only civilly or before a minister of another religion is not considered to have the semblance and form of a true marriage, because such a ceremony is not even regarded as a putative marriage. Thus, an inquiry or investigation of such a previous marriage does not require the use of an actual judicial process for declaring the nullity. In such cases, the only requirement is that the parish priest or the delegate of the Ordinary, through some administrative investigation according to cc. 1066-1067, attains moral certitude concerning the effective free status of the one marrying before she/he is permitted to have a canonical celebration of a sacramental marriage (cf. Pontifical Commission for the Authentic Interpretation of the Code of Canon Law, *Response*, 26 June 1984, n. II, in *AAS*, 76 [1984], p. 747).

For this reason, in the case of a Catholic who celebrates a civil marriage, there is total absence of the canonical form, and consequently, simple convalidation, in the strict sense, cannot be used in such a case.

10. However, there are some who think that the civil marriage of those who are bound to observe the canonical form (cf. 1099 *CIC/17*) can be sanated through simple convalidation because some public form is observed and, therefore, it is a matter of a defect of form rather than an absence of form: "I maintain ... that in our Code the so-called civil marriage may be convalidated (whether in a simple form or in a radical sanation" (G. Montini, "La convalidazione del matrimonio: semplice; sanazione in radice," in *Quaderni della Mendola*, 3, *Matrimonio e disciplina ecclesiastica*, Milano, 1996, p. 192).

L. Chiappetta states: "A *religious* marriage is the one celebrated in the canonical form prescribed by the Church. A *civil* marriage is the one contracted in a form prescribed by the State, before a public magistrate or official. Such a marriage moreover is *legitimate*, if the contractants are not baptized (c. 1015, §3 *CIC/17*); *illegitmate*, if it is attempted by persons bound to the canonical form in accord with the norm of c. 1117" (L. Chiappetta, *Il matrimonio nella nuova legislazione canonica e concordataria, manuale giuridico pastorale*, Roma, Edizioni Dehoniane, 1990, pp. 15-16, n. 34).

"The defect of form can be verified in several ways: absence of a minister competent in virtue of ordinary or delegated faculty (unless the Church 'supplies' the lack of necessary faculty according to the norm of c. 144), absence of witnesses or even of one of them. The civil marriage itself can be regarded as a marriage null because of defect of form" (ibid., p. 400, n. 1160).

Wernz-Vidal, therefore, correctly note: "In virtue of the modern law, in a civil marriage a man and a woman, by means of a true and proper bilateral contract, mutually give to each other certain perpetual right to the use of the body for the purpose of generating and educating the offspring" (Wernz-Vidal, *Ius matrimoniale*, p. 736, n. 583).

Therefore, if the absence of any legitimate form, which can indeed be radically sanated (cf. c. 1139, §1 *CIC/17*), is also admitted under the category of defect of canonical form, simple convalidation would be applicable also to marriages entered into through a civil ritual only.

11. However, as in every case, the illustrious doctor of canon law, Cardinal Urbano Navarrete, after conducting an accurate study of the entire question, has recently reached the following conclusion in the article: "*A proposito del decreto della Segnatura Apostolica del 23 novembre 2005*," in *Periodica*, 96 (2007), p. 333: "Anyway, from whatever has been said so far, the following important conclusion can be drawn: according to the interpretation consistent with all the canons on convalidation and according to the very wording of cc. 1156-1158/83 (cc. 1133-1135/17), the ecclesiastical law concerning the obligation to renew the consent for the validity of simple convalidation, limits itself to the case of nullity 'due to a diriment impediment'. If any confusion should remain, one would at least be certain that this is a question of a doubtful law, and then the first part of c. 14 should be applied, 'Laws, even invalidating and disqualifying ones, do not oblige when there is a doubt of law', a norm that is particularly binding with respect to those who should apply the laws on the administration of justice in the Church, with the prospect of a risk of committing injustice to passive subjects. Precisely for this reason, according to my opinion, in the present state of legislation it is not in conformity with the law in force to demand the renewal of consent, according to the meaning of cc. 1156-1157/83 (cc. 1133-1135/17), in the invalidities 'due to defect of consent' (cc. 1159/93; c. 1136/17), nor in those 'due to defect of form' (c. 1160; c. 1137/17)."

Rotal jurisprudence affirms the same; for example, we read in a sentence *coram* Huber: "In short, we are not dealing in the case before us with the convalidation of an invalid marriage, but with a new canonical celebration of marriage. In fact, as far as the Church in concerned, a civil marriage is by no means regarded as null or putative, because it is deemed to be simply non-existent. For, convalidation is admitted only when a marriage is null because of a canonical cause or defect; but this can in no way be admitted in the case of an inexistent marriage, as in a case of civil marriage. 'Convalidation of marriage is an act by which a marriage that was celebrated before under a legitimate semblance and form, but invalidly, is so restored that it acquires its validity' (Wernz– Vidal, *Ius matrimoniale*, p. 852, n. 652)'.

"Unfortunately, some confusion is created by the fact that in some particular Churches, the expression 'convalidatio' (v.d. 'convalidation') or the expression 'benedictio' (v.d. 'blessing') for canonical marriage celebrated after a prior civil or non-Catholic ceremony, are taken in an improper sense ...

"In a strict sense, therefore, it is lawful in the case to speak of a new celebration of marriage, or, more correctly, of a first (and certainly before the Church, the only) celebration of marriage (decision *c.* Huber, nn. 5-6).

12. Therefore, in order to clear away the inefficacy of a merely civil ceremony, the very same requisites necessary for the first celebration of any marriage of a Catholic party are required, that is to say, actual *de praesenti* consent of the parties, manifested properly through the legitimate canonical form and absence of an obstacle of some diriment impediment. It makes no difference if we call this a first, new or renewed consent, provided that it is clear to everyone that there is an actual, effective matrimonial consent, present at the moment of celebrating the canonical wedding.

For, already in the canonical celebration which clears away the inefficacy of the merely civil celebration (cf. c. 1160), that is, in the first and true nuptial celebration, it is necessary, at least externally, that the words expressing true consent are pronounced. Thus, the condition of that marriage is the same as the one to be fulfilled in every marriage, namely it is governed by the prescript of c. 1101, §1: "The internal consent of the mind is presumed to conform to the words and signs used in celebrating the marriage."

Nor is it permitted, for the sake of creative interpretation and use in a broader sense of the well defined canonical term 'convalidation', to reverse the burden of proof entirely so that the judges and the defender of the bond, instead of the petitioner, are forced to demonstrate the new and renewed consent in the parties, for in this case also, the marriage that was properly celebrated possesses the favour of law (c. 1060).

"Whenever there is a repeated celebration in canonical form of a marriage that was inefficacious because of lack of legitimate form, there is necessarily present, in the very words of the canonical form that is used, a new expression, that is, an external manifestation, of the consent. Hence, it is up to the petitioner to prove that the consent given during the canonical ceremony (and therefore, *de facto* the very new act of consent) was not a true, and actual act of matrimonial consent *de praesenti*. Evidently, the will to give and receive at this moment and from this moment in perpetuity all the essential rights-duties of marriage is considered the consent *de praesenti*. Therefore, *the real question in these cases precisely is whether or not there is total simulation*. For, the nullity in this case is claimed either because it is believed that the party had really not given or received the true matrimonial consent at the moment of canonical celebration, because he/she had remained content with the consent already given during the civil ceremony, or because it is determined that the party had consciously simulated, refusing to present the consent at that moment and unwilling to recognize any efficacy and validity to the canonical ceremony" (decision *c.* Boccafola, 12 March 1998, in *RRT Dec.*, 90 [1999], pp. 233-234, n. 12).

13. It is necessary that consent is legitimately manifested, and for Catholics it is done according to the canonical form (cf. c. 1081, §1 *CIC/17*). Consent is an act of the will, which can turn toward the object of the contract also implicitly.

Total simulation of consent is perpetrated also "by simulation of the matrimonial will," and one who does this "gives no consent to it, because he/she positively did not want to give consent when he/she could have done so, that is, when he/she had the intention not to contract, but, as we usually say, he/she prefers to play act; or more precisely if someone positively excludes the intention to contract, that is, rejects the intention to contract, or someone who completely lacks the matrimonial will" (A. Stankiewicz, "De iurisprudentia rotali recentiore circa simulationem totalem et partialem," in *Monitor ecclesiasticus*, 122 [1997], pp. 210-211).

The matrimonial contract is governed by natural, evangelical and canonical laws; for this reason, the Magisterium of the Church always taught that a marriage between the baptized is indissoluble. The conjugal communion is distinguished not only by its unity but also by its indissolubility: "And this intimate union, as a mutual giving of two persons, and the good of children, demand total fidelity from the spouses and require an unbreakable unity between them" (Second Vatican Council, Constitution on the Church in the Modern World, *Gaudium et spes*, n. 48).

Therefore, canon law received this Magisterial teaching and declares: "The essential properties of marriage are unity and indissolubility, which in Christian marriage obtain a special firmness by reason of the sacrament" (c. 1056).

Also c. 1057, §1 determines: "The consent of the parties, legitimately manifested between persons qualified by law, makes marriage; no human power is able to supply this consent"; for, in celebrating marriage, a truly matrimonial consent is necessary on the part of both spouses; therefore, this consent is necessary to establish marriage with its essential elements. And §2 of the same canon states: "Matrimonial consent is an act of the will by which a man and a woman mutually give and accept each other through an irrevocable consent in order to establish marriage." Especially because, "The matrimonial covenant, by which a man and a woman establish between themselves a partnership of the whole of life and which is ordered by its nature to the good of the spouses and the procreation and education of offspring, has been raised by Christ the Lord to the dignity of a sacrament between the baptized" (c. 1055, §1).

Hence, c. 1101 confirms: "§1. The internal consent of the mind is presumed to conform to the words or signs used in celebrating the marriage. §2. If, however, either or both of the parties by a positive act of the will exclude marriage itself, some essential element of marriage, or some essential property of marriage, the party contracts invalidly."

"Feigning, that is, simulation of matrimonial consent is verified when a contractant externally pronounces seriously and properly the words which express consent, but he/she does not have it internally" (Gasparri, *Tractatus canonicus de matrimonio*, vol. II, p. 36, n. 814).

Simulation is a dissonance between the declaration of the will and the internal will, which impedes the composition of consent, without which marriage cannot arise. Therefore, the act of the will should be sincere.

Simulation consists in a positive act of the will by which a contractant excludes marriage itself, or some essential element or some essential property of marriage. One who simulates consent contracts marriage invalidly and, while he/she externally pronounces the words of consent, internally however by a positive act of the will excludes marriage itself, or all right to conjugal act, or some essential property of marriage (c. 1101, §2).

One who simulates totally does not want to contract marriage; one who excludes some good wants to contract but intends a marriage as conceived by him/her self.

"Therefore, a revocable consent, given for a time only, is not valid to establish marriage, because it denies the right of perpetuity. In fact, indissolubility by its nature does not permit the distinction between the right and its exercise, and a contractant who determines by a positive act of the will to enter into a marriage that is merely dissoluble, to be dissolved according to his/her whim, by that very fact excludes the essential property of indissolubility from matrimonial consent and, therefore, contracts invalidly" (decision *c.* Di Felice, 31 November 1981, in *RRT Dec.*, 73 [1981], p. 530, n. 3).

Simulation by a positive act of the will should be proved in the juridical forum.

14. Canon 1101, §2 of *CIC/83* also states: "If, however, either or both of the parties by a positive act of the will exclude marriage itself ... contracts invalidly."

"Thus, someone can exclude marriage itself not only by refusing, by a positive act of the will, to elicit the internal consent ... but also by pursuing some other end totally alien, that is, extrinsic, to marriage, as the principal and exclusive object of consent; which likewise, although it is less properly called total simulation, juridically assumes a semblance of fiction" (decision *c.* Anné, 13 November 1962, in *RRT Dec.*, 54 [1962], pp. 591-592, n. 2).

Every contract, therefore, even matrimonial contract, has its own cause. And this cause must be diligently "distinguished from the motive by which the contractants are led to enter into a juridic contract, that is, from an extrinsic end.

"The cause of matrimonial contract cannot be anything other than the mutual giving and accepting of the perpetual and exclusive right to the body for acts *per se* apt for the generation and education of offspring ... When this cause is lacking, namely, if a contractant exclusively intends to contract something essentially different from marriage, the matrimonial contract collapses and it is only 'a naked and imaginary' reason, which "is regarded as not being done' ..." (ibid.).

In order to perpetrate this form of simulation, that is, fiction, it is not sufficient to contract solely for some other cause, that is, for an end extrinsic to marriage, but it is necessary that the very object of marriage be simultaneously excluded by a positive act of the will, namely, the true juridic cause of the matrimonial contract, which, according to c. 1101, §2, is called marriage itself.

And the cited sentence *coram* Anné states: "The invalidity of marriage, however, does not follow in case of mere absence of an *explicit intention* to contract marriage. For, the external expression itself becomes consent through the positive act of the will, and 'the internal consent of the mind is always presumed to conform to the words or signs used in celebrating the marriage' (c. 1086, §1), and this presumption cannot be overturned except through proof of a contrary positive act of the will [...]" (ibid.).

Original Latin Text of the In Iure Section: de defectuosa convalidatione

6. Matrimonium facit partium consensus inter personas iure habiles legitime manifestatus, qui nulla potestate humana suppleri valet. Idque tenendum est, attento praescripto sive veteris Codicis Iuris Canonici (can. 1081, §1) sive vigentis (can. 1057, §1). De consensu matrimoniali Paulus VI affirmavit: "Vi huius principii, omnibus probe cogniti, matrimonium exsistit eo ipso temporis momento, quo coniuges matrimonialem consensum praestant iuridice validum ... Quod fit ut, cum semel effectum iuridicum creaverit seu vinculum matrimoniale, huius-

modi consensus irrevocabilis evadat ac virtute careat id, quod peperit, destruendi" (Paulus VI, Allocutio ad Rotam Romanam, diei 9 februarii 1976, in *AAS*, 68 [1976], p. 206).

Si alteruter nubentium catholice baptizatus sit coniugalis consensus praestandus est iuxta canonicam formam (can. 1099 *CIC/17*; can. 1117 *CIC/83*).

7. Matrimonium mere apparens ac invalidum verificari potest cum, iuxta legem canonicam, tripliciter deficere possit iuridicus effectus celebrati matrimonii, cum nempe adfuerit impedimentum dirimens (can. 1133 *CIC/17*; can. 1156 *CIC/83*), vel defuerit ab alterutra parte verus interior consensus (can. 1136 *CIC/17*; can. 1158 *CIC/83*), vel canonica forma observata vitiata fuerit (can. 1137 *CIC/17*; can. 1160 *CIC* 1983).

Cum hisce in casibus invalidum sit matrimonium et coniuges pergant in ducenda cohabitatione, dupliciter cavet canonica lex, scilicet vel per simplicem convalidationem vel per sanationem in radice.

Convalidatio simplex applicatur si matrimonium irritum fuit vel ob impedimentum dirimens vel ob defectum consensus, et nuptiae convalidantur – in casu impedimenti, – per cessationem vel dispensationem impedimenti una cum renovatione consensus saltem illius partis impedimenti consciae in casu defectus consensus –, "si pars quae non consenserat, iam consentiat, dummodo consensus ab altera parte praestitus perseveret" (cfr. can. 1136 §1 *CIC/17*; can. 1159 §1 *CIC/83*); Attamen, si defectus consensus etiam externus fuerit ac probari posset, necesse est ut consensus forma canonica praestetur (can. 1159 §3 *CIC/83*, can. 1136, § 3 *CIC/17*). Similiter, matrimonium irritum ob formam canonicam vitiose celebratam, ut validum fiat, forma canonica contrahi debet (can. 1160 *CIC/83*).

Pro convalidatione simplici, iure ecclesiastico ad validitatem, requiritur renovatio consensus, i.e., ut verum vinculum matrimoniale momento convalidationis oriatur requiritur "novus voluntatis actus in matrimonium quod constet ab initio nullum fuisse" (can. 1134 *CIC/17*). Similiter statuit c. 1156 *CIC/83*.

"Haec renovatio iure ecclesiastico requiritur ad validitatem, etiamsi, initio utraque pars consensum praestiterit nec postea revocaverit" (can. 1333, § 2 *CIC/17*; can. 1156, § 2 *CIC/83*).

8. Nihilominus, quaestio disputatur utrum institutum convalidationis, stricto sensu intellectae, applicetur matrimonio ubi adfuerit totalis carentia requisitae formae canonicae.

Nam si pars catholica matrimonium attentet coram auctoritate civili vel ministro alius religionis (i.e., sine dispensatione a forma canonica), talis celebratio manifeste caret qualicumque elemento formae canonicae ac recte describitur veluti 'matrimonium inexistens', cum nullo modo habet speciem vel figuram veri matrimonii.

In casu matrimonii civilis baptizatorum in Ecclesia catholica vel in eamdem receptorum, si iure vigenti actu formali ab ea non defecerint (can. 1117 *CIC/83*), matrimonium utique nullum est et patet nullitatem pendere ex defectu debitae formae, sed plures periti in lege canonica potius de matrimonio inexsistenti, in casu, loqui malunt.

Longa traditio canonica, ut testatur scriptis plurium auctorum re vera peritorum in re canonica, tenet, sensu stricto, locutionem ac institutum "convalidationis" nullo modo applicari potest nuptiis partis catholicae mere civiliter celebratis ac sine observantia formae canonicae. Nam requisitum fundamentale ac terminus a quo ut convalidatio sit applicanda, est semper matrimonium invalidum; matrimonium catholicae partis mere civiliter celebratum, sine dispensatione a forma canonica, haud implet praecisam definitionem matrimonii invalidi quia tale civile matrimonium nullo modo habeat speciem vel figuram veri matrimonii.

"Matrimonii convalidatio est actus quo id quod matrimonii veri nonnisi speciem habebat, tale fit reapse, suppleto quod ad hoc ei antea deerat" (T. Vlaming, *Praelectiones iuris canonici*, vol. II, p. 349, n. 760). Et ita: "Simplex matrimonii convalidatio est actus quo matrimonium invalidum redditur validum cum renovato consensu" (P. Gasparri, *Tractatus canonicus de matrimonio*, ed. nova ad mentem *Codicis I.C.*, vol. II, In Civitate Vaticana, Typis polyglottis Vaticanis, 1932, p. 253, n. 1189);

"Convalidatio matrimonii est actus quo matrimonium ante praescripta forma celebratum, at invalidum ob aliquod vitium ipsius formae vel consensus, vel ob aliquod impedimentum dirimens, sanatur et validum fit. Non habetur proinde proprie dicta convalidatio nisi habeatur saltem species veri matrimonii. Nec item sermo esse potest de convalidatione si agatur de matrimonio valide sed solum illicite celebrato" (M. Conte a Coronata, *Institutiones iuris canonici ad usum utriusque cleri et scholarum. De sacramentis tractatus canonicus*, tomus III, *De matrimonio et de sacramentalibus*, 3a ed., Romae, Marietti, 1957, p. 933).

Simili modo Wernz– Vidal: "Convalidatio matrimonii est actus quo matrimonium ante sub legitima specie et forma, sed nulliter celebratum, ita restauratur ut suum consequatur valorem" (F.X. Wernz – P. Vidal, *Ius canonicum*, tomus V, *Ius matrimoniale*, 3a ed., Romae, Apud Aedes Universitatis Gregorianae, 1946, p. 852, n. 652).

Ita iuxta A.C. Jemolo: "... oggi certo che il matrimonio civile dei cattolici é per la Chiesa inesistente come matrimonio, e non già nullo per difetto di forma, sicche non puo parlarsi di convalidazione semplice. Tra i cattolici, il canone può quindi avere applicazione solo nei casi di matrimonio nullo per essere stato contratto dinanzi ad un vescovo o ad un parroco che celebrasse fuori del suo territorio, o che versasse in alcuna delle condizioni indicate nel can. 1095, §1, o ad un sacerdote privo di licenza o con licenza nulla o sottoposta a condizione non verificatasi, o senza la presenza dei testimoni" (A.C. Jemolo, *Il matrimonio nel diritto canonico*, Milano, Francesco Varaldi, 1941, p. 307, n. 165).

"Pro Jemolo igitur, si bene intelligimus eius mentem, in casu matrimonii mere civilis catholicorum, convalidatio non tantum non habet locum, sed nec habere potest cum, in casu, nullatenus de una vera prima matrimonii celebratione loquendum est. Aliis verbis canon applicandus est ubi vitiosa fuerit forma, non autem ubi omnino absens" (decisio coram Funghini, diei 30 iunii 1988, in *RRT Dec.*, 80 [1988], pp. 440-441, n. 2).

Etiam F. Galtier, orientali sermone doctus, affirmat: "On convalide un mariage invalide; l' absence de mariage n'est pas un mariage nul. On ne peut donc parler de convalidation quand il s'agit de regulariser la situation de deux personnes qui se sont installées dans la concubinage" (F. Gaitier, *Le mariage: discipline orientale et discipline occidentale*, [Beyrouth, Université St. Joseph, Faculté de Théologie], 1950, p. 357).

Quibus attentis absolute loqui de matrimonio civili uti inexistenti pro Ecclesia arduum videtur eo vel magis quod idem, dummodo initum fuerit affectu maritali et consensus sub specie et figura extrinseca iusti matrimonii datus perseveret, iuxta canonem 1139, §1 *CIC/17*, sanari potest in radice.

Ad mentem citati canonis dicendum proinde rectius agi de matrimonio iuridice inefficaci.

Sine negotio admitti enim potest contrahentes, quamvis in eccl esia catholica baptizatos vel ad eam ex haeresi aut schismate conversos, coram magistratu civili revera velle fieri pro foro interno et externo veri coniuges. Eorum vero consensus, qui naturaliter sufficiens esset, est iuridice inefficax:

deficiente necessaria forma canonica, quibus iidem vi canonis 1099, §1 *CIC/17* (c. 1162, §1 *CIC/83*) sub poena nullitatis matrimonii obstringuntur.

9. Mens Legislatoris dein excludere videtur convalidationem simplicem pro matrimoniis civilibus, quia in ipsis abest prorsus forma canonica.

Nam, in schemate anni 1980 redacto a Pontificia Commissione Codici Iuris Canonici Recognoscendo, in can. 1014, qui respondet can. 1061 Codicis nunc vigentis, edicebatur: "§4. Matrimonium invalidum intelligitur etiam matrimonium civiliter contractum, quod est propter defectum formae canonicae invalidum." Attamen, deinde haec paragraphus delata est, atque ad rem Secretaria respondit: "Ad §4: Supprimitur, nam revera potest ad conclusiones erroneas ducere, neque eius omissio obstat sanationi in radice quae concedi potest etiam si matrimonium sit nullum" (*Communicationes*, 15 [1983], p. 224).

Et reapse Codex vigens pro sanatione in radice loquitur de non servata forma canonica "a forma canonica, si servata non fuerit" (can. 1161, § 1), cum vero in convalidatione simplici habeatur figura "defectus formae" (cf. can. 1160), distinctione allata inter absentiam formae canonicae et defectum formae canomcae.

Ideo, etiam in vigente Codice, partis catholicae matrimonium tantummodo civiliter vel apud ministrum alius religionis celebratum haud censetur habere figuram ac speciem veri matrimonii, cum talis caerimonia ne putativum quidem matrimonium consideretur. Ita, inquisitio vel investigatio de aliquo tali priore matrimonio minime requirit usum actualis processus iudicialis pro declaranda nullitate; in talibus casibus requiritur tantummodo ut parochus vel delegatus Ordinarii per aliquam investigationem administrativam iuxta cann. 1066-1067 se moraliter certum reddat de effectivo statu libero nupturientis, antequam ei permittatur canonica celebratio Sacramenti matrimonii (cfr. Responsio Pontificiae Commissionis pro Codici Iuris Canonici Authentice Interpretando, diei 26 iunii 1984, n. II, in *AAS*, 76 [1984], p. 747).

In casu ergo catholici qui matrimonium civile celebrat, totalis absentia formae canonicae habetur, ac proinde convalidatio – simplex, stricto sensu, in huiusmodi casu haberi nequit.

10. Attamen, sunt aliqui qui censent matrimonium civile illorum qui ad formam canonicam servandam astricti sunt (cf. 1099 *CIC* 1917) per convalidationem simplicem sanari posse, quia in ipso aliqua forma publica servata est, ac proinde de defectu formae canonicae agitur, potius quam de absentia formae: "Ritengo ... che nel nostro codice il c.d. matrimonio civile sia convalidabile (sia in forma semplice sia in sanazione in radice)" (G. Montini, "La convalidazione del matrimonio: semplice; sanazione in radice," in *Quaderni della Mendola*, 3: *Matrimonio e disciplina ecclesiastica*, Milano, 1996, p. 192).

Aloisius Chiappetta affirmat: "Il matrimonio **religioso** è quello celebrato nella forma canonica prescritta dalla Chiesa. Il matrimonio **civile** [è] quello contratto nella forma prescritta dallo Stato, dinanzi al pubblico magistrato o funzionario. Tale matrimonio è per altro *legittimo*, se i contraenti non sono battezzati (can. 1015, §3 *CIC/17*); *illegittimo*, se attentato da persone tenute alla forma canonica, a norma del can. 1117" (L. Chiappetta, *Il matrimonio nella nuova legislazione canonica e concordataria, manuale giuridico-pastorale*, Roma, Edizioni Dehoniane, 1990, p. 400, n. 1160).

"Il difetto di forma può verificarsi in più modi: assenza del ministro competente per facoltà ordinaria o delegata (tranne che la Chiesa 'supplisca' la mancanza della facoltà necessaria, a norma del can. 144), assenza dei testimoni o anche di uno di essi. Lo stesso matrimonio civile può essere considerato un matrimonio nullo per difetto di forma" (ibid., pp. 15-16, n. 34).

Recte igitur animadverterat Wernz–Vidal: "Ex iure moderno in matrimonio civili vir et mulier vero et proprio contractu bilaterali sibi mutuo tradunt ius quoddam perpetuum ad usum corporis in ordine ad generandam et educandam prolem" (Wernz-Vidal, *Ius matrimoniale*, p. 736, n. 583).

Si ergo etiam absentia cuiuslibet legitimae formae, quae quidem in radice sanari potest (cfr. can. 1139, §1 *CIC/17*), sub categoria defectus formae canonicae reciperetur, etiam ad matrimonia, tantum per ritum civilem inita, convalidatio simplex pertineret.

11. Utcumque ac in omni casu, illustris doctor iuris canonici, Urbanus Cardinalis Navarrete, post accuratum examen totius quaestionis, nuper hanc conclusionem pertingit, scribens in articulo, "A proposito del decreto della Segnatura Apostolica del 23 novembre 2005," in *Periodica*, 96 (2007), p. 333: "Ad ogni modo da quanto detto risulta questa conclusione importante: secondo l'interpretazione congruente con tutti i canoni sulla convalidazione e secondo pure la lettera stessa dei cann. 1156-1158/83 (cann. 1133-1135/17), la legge ecclesiastica sull'obbligo di rinnovare il consenso per la validità della convalidazione semplice, si limita soltanto al caso di nullità 'ob impedimentum dirimens'. Se restasse qualche perplessità, per lo meno sarebbe certo che si tratta di una legge dubbia, e allora si deve applicare la prima parte del can. 14, 'Leges etiam irritantes ed inhabilitantes in dubio iuris non urgent', norma che è particolarmente obbligante rispetto a coloro che debbono applicare le leggi riguardanti l'amministrazione della giustizia nella Chiesa, sotto il rischio di commettere ingiustizie ai soggetti passivi. Proprio per questo, a mio parere, nello stato attuale della legislazione non è conforme al diritto vigente esigere la rinnovazione del consenso, ai sensi dei cann. 1156-1157/83 (cann. 1133- 1135/17), nelle invalidità 'ob defectum consensus' (can. 1159/83; can. 1136/17) ne in quelle 'ob defectum formae' (cann. 1160/83; can. 1137/17)."

Idem affirmat jurisprudentia Rotalis, e. g. in sententia coram Huber: "In specie nostra, prorsus, haud agitur de convalidatione invalidi matrimonii, sed de nova matrimonii canonica celebratione. Matrimonium civile, enim, pro Ecclesia minime nullum vel putativum retinetur, quia simpliciter inexistens putatur. Convalidatio etenim admittitur solummodo cum matrimonium, ob causam vel vitium canonicum, nullum sit; at hoc minime dari potest in casu matrimonii inexistentis, sicut in casu matrimonii civilis: 'Convalidatio matrimonii est actus quo matrimonium ante sub legitima specie et forma, sed nulliter celebratum, ita restauratur, ut suum consequatur valorem' (Wernz – Vidal, *Ius matrimoniale*, p. 852, n. 652).

"Proh dolor aliqua confusio gignitur ex facto quod in aliquibus Ecclesiis particularibus, vox 'convalidatio' (v.d. 'convalidation') vel vox 'benedictio' (v.d. 'blessing') pro matrimoniis canonicis celebratis post aliquam praehabitam caeremoniam civilem vel non catholicam, sensu improprio sumuntur ...'

"Stricto sensu, igitur, fas est in casu loqui de nova matrimonii celebratione, vel, rectius, de prima (et quidem in facie Ecclesiae, unica) matrimonii celebratione (sententia coram Huber, nn. 5-6).

12. Ideo, pro inefficacita merae civilis caerimoniae purganda requiruntur illa eadem requisita utpote pro prima celebratione qualiscumque matrimonii partis catholicae, i.e., actualis consensus de praesenti partium, rite manifestatus per legitimam formam canonicam atque absentia obicis alicuius impedimenti dirimentis. Nihil differt si nominemus hunc consensum primum, novum vel renovatum, dummodo omnibus palam sit adesse actualem, effectivum consensum matrimonialem, praesentem momento celebrationis canonicarum nuptiarum.

Nam iam in canonica celebratione quae purget inefficacitatem celebrationis merae civilis (cfr. c. 1160), seu in prima ac vera celebratione nuptiali, requiritur, saltern modo exteriore, pronuntiatio verborum verum consensum exprimentium. Ita, conditio illius matrimonii est eadem ac illa quae pro omni matrimonio adimplenda est, scilicet regitur praescriptione c. 1101: "Internus animi consensus praesumitur conformis verbis vel signis in celebrando matrimonio adhibitis."

Nec licet, gratia creativae interpretationis ac usus in sensu largiore iam bene determinati termini canonici 'convalidationis', omnino obvertere onus probandi ita ut dein, in vice actoris, iudicibus vel Defensori vinculi oporteat demonstrare novum ac renovatum consensum in partibus, nam etiam in hoc casu, matrimonium rite celebratum gaudet favore iuris (c. 1060).

"Quotiescumque enim habetur iterata celebratio in forma canonica nuptiarum inefficacium ob carentiam legitimae formae, necessarie adest, ex ipsissimis verbis formae canonicae celebratae adhibitis, nova expressio, seu externa manifestatio, consensus. Exinde remanet actori demonstrare consensum traditum in caerimonia canonica (ac proinde, de facto, ipsum novum actum consensus) haud fuisse verum, et actualem actum consensus matrimonialis de praesenti. Consensus de praesenti, scilicet, consideratur voluntas tradendi ac accipiendi hoc momento atque ab hoc momento usque in perpetuum omnia iura-officia essentialia matrimonialia. Ideoque, *vera quaestio in his casibus est praecise utrum adsit vel non totalis simulatio consensus.* Nam nullitas in casu postulatur sive quia censetur partem haud revera tradidisse vel accepisse verum consensum matrimonialem momento celebrationis canonicae, cum tranquille quieverit consensui iam in caerimonia civili dato, sive quia aestimatur partem conscie simulavisse, refutantem praestare consensum illo momento atque nolentem recognoscere ullam efficacitatem ac validitatem caerimoniae canonicae" (decisio *c.* Boccafola, diei martii 1998, in *RRT Dec.*, 90 [1999], pp. 233-234, n. 12)

DE SIMULATIONE

13. Consensus quidem manifestetur legitime, et pro catholicis iuxta formam canonicam, opus est (cfr. can. 1081, §1 *CIC/17*); consensus est actus voluntatis, qui etiam implicite in obiectum contractus vertere potest.

Simulatio totalis consensus quidem patratur etiam "per simulationem voluntatis matrimonialis," et hoc facit "qui nullum in idem consensum praestat, cum noluerit positive, dum posset, consensum praestare, seu cum animum habet non contrahendi, sed, ut dici solet, comoediam agere mavult; vel pressius si quis positive excludit animum contrahendi, seu reicit intentionem contrahendi, aut cui deest matrimonialis voluntas" (A. Stankiewicz, "De iurisprudentia rotali recentiore circa simulationem totalem et partialem," in *Monitor ecclesiasticus*, 122 [1997], pp. 210-211).

Contractus matrimonialis regitur legibus naturalibus, evangelicis et canonicis, idcirco Magisterium Ecclesiae semper docuit matrimonium inter baptizatos esse indissolubile. Coniugalis communio non solum unitate sua est insignis, sed etiam indissolubilitate: "Quae intima unio, utpote mutua duarum personarum donatio, sicut et bonum liberorum, plenam coniugum fidem exigunt et indissolubilem eorum unitatem urgent" (Concilium Vaticanum Secundum, Const. Past. *Gaudium et spes*, n. 48).

Quapropter lex canonica hanc Magisterii doctrinam recepit et edicit: "Essentiales matrimonii proprietates sunt unitas et indissolubilitas, quae in matrimonio christiano ratione sacramenti peculiarem obtinent firmitatem" (can. 1056).

Etiam can. 1057, §1 statuit: "Matrimonium facit partium consensus inter personas iure habiles legitime manifestatus, qui nulla potestate humana suppleri valet," nam, in celebrando coniugio, requiritur consensus vere matrimonialis ex parte utriusque nupturientis, quapropter hic consensus sit oportet ad constituendum connubium cum eiusdem essentialibus elementis. Atque eiusdem canonis §2 statuit: "Consensus matrimonialis est actus voluntatis, quo vir et mulier foedere irrevocabili sese mutuo tradunt et accipiunt ad constituendum matrimonium." Praesertim quia: "Matrimoniale foedus, quo vir et mulier inter se totius vitae consortium constituunt, indole sua naturali ad bonum coniugum atque ad prolis generationem et educationem ordinatum, a Christo Domino ad sacramenti dignitatem inter baptizatos evectum est" (can. 1055, §1).

Exinde can. 1101 sancit: "§1. Internus animi consensus praesumitur conformis verbis vel signis in celebrando matrimonio adhibitis. § 2. At si alterutra vel utraque pars positivo voluntatis actu excludat matrimonium ipsum vel matrimonii essentiale aliquod elementum, vel essentialem aliquam proprietatem, invalide contrahit.."

"Fictio seu simulatio consensus matrimonialis tunc verificatur, quando contrahens externe quidem verba consensum exprimentia serio et rite profert, sed interne illum non habet" (Gasparri, *Tractatus canonicus de matrimonio*, vol. II, p. 36, n. 814).

Simulatio est discordia inter declarationem voluntatis et internam voluntatem, quae impedit compositionem consensus, sine quo matrimonium oriri non potest. Ita actus voluntatis debet esse sincerus.

Simulatio consistit in positivo actu voluntatis, quo nupturiens excludit matrimonium ipsum, vel matrimonii essentiale aliquod elementum vel essentialem aliquam proprietatem. Invalide matrimonium contrahit qui consensum simulat et, dum consensus verba externe profert, interne autem positivo voluntatis actu excludit matrimonium ipsum, aut omne ius ad coniugalem actum, vel essentialem aliquam matrimonii proprietatem (can. 1101 §2).

Qui totaliter simulat, ipse nullum vult contrahere matrimonium, qui excludit aliquod bonum, vult contrahere sed intendit matrimonium utpote a se conceptum.

"Consensus ideo revocabilis, solummodo ad tempus praestitus, haud validus est ad matrimonium constituendum, quia ius perpetuitatis coniugii denegat. Etenim indissolubilitas suapte natura distinctionem iuris ab eiusdem exercitio non permittit atque nupturiens, positivo voluntatis actu statuens coniugium mere solubile inire iuxta suum arbitrium solvendum, eo ipso excludit essentialem proprietatem indissolubilitatis e matrimoniali consensu ac proinde invalide contrahit" (decisio coram Di Felice, diei 31 novembris 1981, in *RRT Dec.*, 73 [1981], p. 530, n. 3).

Simulatio per positivum actum voluntatis in foro iudiciali probari debet.

14. Etiam statuit can. 1101 §2 *CIC/83*: "Si alterutra vel utraque pars positivo voluntatis actu excludit matrimonium ipsum ... invalide contrahit."

"Ita, ipsum matrimonium excludere quidam potest, non tantum renuendo, actu positivo voluntatis, consensum internum ponere ... sed etiam prosequendo alium finem a matrimonio omnino alienum seu extrinsecum tamquam obiectum principale et exclusivum consensus; quod pariter, quamvis minus proprie simulatio totalis nuncupatur, potius iuridice speciem fictionis induit" (decisio coram Anné, diei 13 novembris 1962, in *RRT Dec.*, 54 [1962], pp. 591-592, n. 2).

Omnis contractus ideoque et matrimonialis contractus habet suam causam. Quae causa sedulo "distinguenda est a motivo quo contrahentes ad negotium iuridicum ineundum ducuntur seu a fine extrinseco. Causa matrimonialis contractus esse nequit nisi mutua traditio et acceptatio iuris in corpus perpetuum et exclusivum in ordine ad actus per se aptos ad prolis generationem et educationem ... Hac deficiente causa, nempe si contrahens aliud paciscendum exclusive intendit a matrimonio essentialiter diversum, ruit contractus matrimonialis et est tantum 'nuda et imaginaria' ratio, quae 'pro non facta est' ..." (ibid.).

Ad hanc speciem simulationis totalis seu fictionis patrandam non sufficit nuptias contrahere ex sola alia causa seu ob finem matrimonio extrinsecum, sed requiritur, ut simul excludatur actu postivo voluntatis obiectum ipsum matrimonii, nempe vera causa iuridica contractus matrimonialis, quae iuxta can. 1101 §2, ipsum matrimonium nuncupatur.

Et statuit citata sententia coram Anne: "Non sequitur autem invaliditas matrimonii in casu merae absentiae *intentionis explicitae* contrahendi matrimonium. Nam ipsa expressio externa consensus fit per actum positivum voluntatis et 'internus animi consensus semper praesumitur conformis verbis vel signis in celebrando matrimonio adhibitis', (can. 1086 §1), quae praesumptio refelli nequit nisi per probationem actus positivi voluntatis contrarii [...]" (ibid.).

3 — The Argument

15. First of all, we must distinguish by the following observations: a) In the first process before the Tribunal of Smyrna, there were three grounds of nullity: defect of discretion of judgment on the part of the petitioner, and also "defective convalidation" on the part of both parties. The decision in the first grade of jurisdiction was affirmative only in favor of "defective convalidation" on the part of the respondent, who presented an appeal to the Roman Rota against only the affirmative part of the sentence, that is, against the ground of "defective convalidation." b) By its decree, the Rotal *Turnus* admitted the cause to an ordinary examination of the second grade and, because the respondent had appealed against the affirmative part of the sentence, the ground of "defective convalidation" on the part of the woman was the only ground determined in the second grade, and the doubt was formulated as follows: "*Whether there is proof nullity of marriage in the case due to defect of a new act of the will on the part of the woman respondent in convalidating the marriage (can. 1156, §2; 1157).*" c) In fact, such a formulation of the doubt is incorrect for another reason, because it cites only the canons of the present Code of Canon Law; but the marriage in question was celebrated under the 1917 Code of Canon Law, that is to say, in accord with the norm of c. 1099, §1,1° of that law, and this canon obliges all persons baptized in the Catholic Church to observe the canonical form in contracting marriage; and this form is established in c. 1094 of the 1917 Code: "Only those marriages are valid which are contracted before the pastor, or the local Ordinary, or a priest delegated by either of them and at least two witnesses ..."

Because the Rotal *Turnus* had confirmed the sentence rendered at the first grade;

because the Supreme Tribunal of the Apostolic Signatura has granted a new proposition of the cause in the case, we must now proceed before this Apostolic Tribunal according to the norm of c. 1640 of the Code of Canon Law considered together with articles 267, §§2 and 3; 293, §2, of the Instruction *Dignitas connubii*;

having seen the appeal of the respondent against the affirmative part of the sentence at the first grade, that is, against the ground of "defective convalidation";

having seen the concession of the Supreme Tribunal of the Apostolic Signatura of a new proposition of the cause concerning the existence or not of the convalidation of matrimonial consent on the part of the woman respondent;

The present Rotal *Turnus* should determine the doubt according to the only ground that was appealed and according to the concession of the proposition by the Supreme Tribunal of the Apostolic Signatura given concerning the existence or not of the convalidation of matrimonial consent on the part of the woman respondent. Therefore, the doubt was determined under this formula: "*Whether there is proof of nullity of marriage in the case on the ground of defect of convalidation of matrimonial consent on the part of the woman respondent.*"

However, the petitioner could appeal in the future against the grounds negatively dismissed in the first grade of jurisdiction, that is, against the defect of discretion of judgment and against the defect of the convalidation of consent on the part of the same petitioner.

16. The parties first contracted a civil marriage and three months later they celebrated a religious wedding.

The marriage lasted several years and several children were born of the union. The breakup of the marriage must be attributed to the infidelities of the petitioner, who also sought a civil divorce and then married his lover. However, the respondent, who is a very devout Catholic, preserved conjugal fidelity, because "if I didn't feel I was married I would have done the same thing he did."

The woman respondent strenuously opposed the declaration of nullity of the marriage and did not understand, "what I might have said in the (preliminary) deposition that I gave that might make anyone assume that I did not take the vows seriously." And she added: "If I had not thought that in order to be truly married to my husband Brian I needed to be married in the church, I would not have taken the vows."

The woman repeated: "I took the vows seriously and thought they were valid when I made them, just as I consider them to be valid now." And besides, "There was no pressure from any source to marry within the church. The decision to do so was totally ours."

The woman evidently still considers herself validly married in the Church.

17. It is evident from the acts that the woman had loved the petitioner very much. She said: "I mean, I was so enamored with this guy, you know, he was my whole life." And the brother of the petitioner fully confirms this: "She had an incredible crush on him but he did not with her. He did not reciprocate."

The woman distinguishes quite well between a civil and religious marriage.

She argues that she was fully aware of the marriage that was celebrated before the Church: "I have never stopped loving my husband ... Because we were married in the Church, I never felt that I could remarry."

In fact, in celebrating the religious marriage, "Fr. Concessao had us say all our marriage vows again and blessed us. I mean they were the same words that the other man had asked us. Except, he blessed us and then we could go to communion and stuff."

To the question of the judge: "Did you mean them when you said them again?", the respondent replied: "Yeah. I wouldn't have said them otherwise. I mean I would have done it twice if I didn't mean it."

Note the manifestation of the true matrimonial consent of the respondent, although she had to add: "As far as I was concerned, I was already married."

18. The respondent repeatedly confessed that she wanted to be Brian Cabrini's wife; and she in fact states that she had intended to accept conjugal duties in both ceremonies, civil as well as religious: "What Fr. Concessao would do in the Church was to sanctify our marriage vows. Seeing that Brian was going to be posted overseas, we wanted everything 'taken care of' in case he was killed so that we could meet each other in heaven. In both the ceremonies of marriage I had with Brian, I never had any reservations about the permanence of the vows I was taking or that I could ever get out of the marriage."

The woman reports that she had decided together with her spouse to enter into a canonical marriage after they had celebrated the civil ceremony both because Brian was going to be posted overseas where a war was being fought, and because they wanted to avoid any conflict with the man's mother: "We wanted to be married because he was going to go. And she didn't want him to marry me ... So we went and we got married at the justice of the peace ... Then when he was supposed to go overseas, that's when we went to Fr. Concessao ... because Brian's mother didn't want us to get married ... I was going to marry this man. I had a ring from him. We had talked about it. We wanted children. We wanted to be together ... we wanted to get everything straight."

19. The woman's conviction that she had contracted marriage twice does not stand in the way of the validity of the religious marriage: "I felt I was his wife in the time that we were married by a justice of the peace, and the same words that the justice of the peace said to us, were the exact same ones Fr. Concessao said. So to me it was that, I was just kind of doing it all over again."

The distinction of the religious marriage from the civil marriage has been expressed by the respondent many times and in various words: "It just seemed to me that it just straightened all out"; "it gave sanctity to the vows we had made.

And kind of to me I thought, 'Well, you must love me a lot. You're marrying me twice' ... it made it all straight with everybody ... with God, ... with everybody ... my father was happier, because they're very Catholic ..."

The woman knew that "the approval of the Church" was lacking in the civil marriage. She defined the religious marriage: "Just like the frosting on the cake." And still: "At the time we wanted the marriage sanctified by the Church as my husband Brian was about to be sent overseas to fight in the war." For, "seeing that Brian was going overseas to fight, we wanted everything 'taken care of' in case he was killed so that we could meet each other in heaven."

20. The religious celebration, was in fact, sought out by both parties, and the respondent even asked for permission from her Pastor: "We went to Fr. Concessao ... I had to get a dispensation from our parish of Our Lady of Hope," and she even signed the documents of the matrimonial process: "We filled out some papers."

Juliana Brown diligently recalls the absolutely private ceremony: "He made arrangements to be married on a date that ... Father could marry us, in the little chapel. There in St. Joseph. And my sister and her fiancé stood up for us."

According to what we have recalled in the law section, the nullity may be proven if a party has really not given or received the true matrimonial consent at the moment of canonical celebration, because he/she had remained content with the consent already given during the civil ceremony, or if a party consciously simulated, refusing to present the consent at that moment and unwilling to recognize any efficacy and validity to the canonical ceremony.

The woman, as we have seen, really gave and received a true matrimonial consent at the moment of the canonical celebration: "I wouldn't have said them otherwise. I mean I wouldn't have done it twice if I didn't mean it."

The woman, therefore, was not content with the consent already given in the civil ceremony, but she again, that is, "twice," gave consent. Nor did she consciously simulate, but she deeply loved the petitioner, she freely manifested her consent "twice" and acknowledged the full efficacy and validity of the canonical ceremony, as it has emerged from all of the acts of the cause.

Therefore, one cannot say that the respondent fought for the validity of the civil marriage, as the sentence of the first grade stated erroneously based on a Rotal sentence *coram* Rogers: "A person who not only is unaware of the invalidity of the prior marriage but really fights for its validity is that much more certainly prevented from positing a new consent."

Also the Rotal sentence of the second grade did not reach a correct conclusion: "If indeed, while the woman fights, and even strenuously, for the validity of the civil bond, then there is absolutely no possibility for arguing that she had given a new consent in the canonical celebration, which was intended by her at the most as a shadow only to simply confirm the civil union she had celebrated before."

Therefore, it is not possible to accept the affirmation of the same sentence: "... the mind and the will of the woman was altogether extraneous and foreign to marry the man, because she thought that she was already married."

21. In fact, the woman sincerely believed that she was validly married to the man already on the day the civil marriage was celebrated. But, she added: "I quite frankly considered myself married to him from the very moment that we had any sexual activity, which was about a month and a half before we were married." She repeated this statement before the judge: "... I honestly, truthfully felt married to Brian from the time that we were intimate."

The woman, without any knowledge of canon law, wanted only to signify by those words that, by their very first sexual intercourse, she considered herself firmly joined to the man she loved, as if united in marriage. Certainly not united by a civil union, "which she in fact contracted before a civil official," as the Rotal decree erroneously interpreted the woman's confession."

In celebrating the religious marriage, the woman certainly had the intention at least "of doing what the Church does," which is sufficient for a contractant to enter into a valid marriage before the Church

A distinction seems to have been made by the respondent between a civil marriage and a marriage before the Church, as if she had not manifested her marital consent during the religious ceremony: "I've stayed and gone along with the Church's rule because I felt I was married ... first he marries me then he gets sanctified by the Church"; but she notes that the same words of conjugal consent were expressed in both ceremonies implicitly asserting that she had expressed the same words of the conjugal consent also before the sacred minister: "Fr. Concessao had us say all our marriage vows again and blessed us. I mean they were the same words that the other man had asked us. Except, he blessed us and then we could go to communion and stuff."

In her observations after the publication of the acts, the woman declares that her true marriage happened before the Church, and this proves that she really gave her consent for the marriage before the assisting priest: "The church marriage was the real marriage"; and she shows her will to celebrate the canonical marriage because she took the initiative: "His mother did not make the arrangements. We went in person, and spoke to Fr. Concessao ... I prepared for marriage."

The woman also declares in candid words that she chose to celebrate the marriage in the church: "It's not true that it was Brian's mother's insistence that we got married in the Church."

22. The principal question concerns the intention of the respondent in the act of the canonical celebration, because it appears that, for her, her marriage was present already in the act of the civil celebration, and in fact she intended to give herself to the man when she had the first sexual intercourse with him: "I honestly, truthfully felt married to Brian from the time that we were intimate ... I was already married."

She confessed to the interviewing judge that she had not elicited a new consent; according to the woman, the religious rite had completed the act performed before the civil magistrate: "Just like the frosting on the cake."

However, the will to elicit the act with knowledge and awareness is evident from the concise description: "I remember sitting down in this little room. You go in St. Joseph's ... We came back, we signed these papers that he had us fill out ... We discussed getting married in the Church. He had us fill out papers. We signed them. He explained what we were signing. That's when we made the appointment to get married. Approximately two weeks later, we got married."

Both noted something new after the canonical celebration of the marriage, because it was only after the wedding was celebrated in the church that they established their cohabitation and went on a honeymoon: "We took a week and a half honeymoon together after the Church marriage ... we had no honeymoon after our civil marriage." "So it had to be that we got the little apartment, probably in May."

In fact, Juliana had understood the Christian meaning of the celebration of marriage: "I would have encouraged him as strongly as possible, to go and get married in the Church, ... the approval of the Church ... if you weren't finished and married in the Church, and something happened to him, where would he be? I couldn't be with him"; and she gave the wedding ring to the man only during the religious celebration: "I went and bought Brian the wedding ring, and that was the first time he wore the ring, when I put it on his finger."

23. The defect of matrimonial consent on the part of the woman at the moment of the canonical celebration of her marriage is not proven from the acts of the cause.

a) First of all, there is no judicial confession of the simulating party. The woman never confessed that she did not want to renew consent. For, the woman wanted to celebrate the marriage with the man she loved before the Church; she freely expressed her consent before the priest.

The explanation of the second instance sentence of the Rota in support of its own thesis concerning the absence of a true consent is that the woman did not give, according to the judges, a new, that is, a renewed consent. Nevertheless, in each case the consent was truly present at that time of the mutual giving over, because it would have been expressed in the liturgical formula, and no reason is given for considering its exclusion through a positive act of the will of the woman. No reason in fact is put forth for asserting such a tenacious adherence of the woman to her consent given already in the civil ceremony so that she would have felt compelled to feign and to exclude her consent during the canonical wedding. One could think of this in the case of a non-Catholic or non-religious person, who does not want to submit self in any way to the governance of the Church. However, in our case, the opinion of the woman concerning the integrity and validity of a merely civil marriage is only a simple error which did not in any way determine her will.

The words of the woman used before the judge express in popular language simple "feelings" of a person who was completely devoid of any knowledge of canon law. Her understanding of the origin of the marital bond from the sexual relationships she had, cannot be accepted by us as a juridic fact; nor her understanding of the true marital affection arisen from a mere civil celebration.

b) There is no extra-judicial confession on the part of the one simulating.

The man knows nothing about the exclusion of consent in the woman at that moment. The man spoke of some formality in accepting the religious marriage, in order to confirm the civil ceremony, but he knows nothing concerning the woman's intention: "I was going through this marriage in the Church because it was part of the formality and it was to please my mom and dad ... It was just something that had to be done ... I did not consider that a new union was created. .. I felt that the Church service confirmed the civil ceremony ... I have no idea how my former spouse felt at the time." The woman never confessed to her spouse, throughout their marriage, that she refused internal assent while she was pronouncing her matrimonial consent in the canonical form.

The witnesses are not able to report anything about the intention of the woman.

One witness expresses only his personal opinion: "I don't think it meant one thing to her," and in fact the same witness reports that Juliana was stubborn in her will to marry Brian: "I think her main thing was marrying Brian." The wife of that witness also spoke of the same will, although she had known her only after she had been married: "I've heard that she wanted to marry Brian and she made up her mind that's what she was going to do and she'd do it any way she could."

Another witness, one of the petitioner's siblings, who was fourteen years old at the time of the wedding, reports with utmost honesty, that he had never spoken with the respondent concerning the significance she had attributed to the religious celebration of marriage, and he thinks that the customs of that age had played an important role in the choice of the religious celebration after the civil ceremony had already been performed.

The witness Frank Samure also reports that the respondent was firm in her intention to marry the petitioner: "She also said that she was not going to wait the length of time to get married that Brian wanted ... I know she became pregnant on purpose ... she was not going to wait until Brian had completed college to get married."

Another witness only adds general information concerning the circumstances of place and time in which the parties celebrated their marriage.

In fact, the woman herself states: "... when I married my husband 41 years ago, I did so because I loved him, I did so in good faith. I still care for him and consider him my husband." Many times the woman affirms that she wanted to renew her matrimonial consent: "I was doing it over again," and "in both ceremonies of marriage I had with Brian, I never had any reservations about the permanence of the vows I was taking..."

c) There are no proofs in support of any reason proportionate to the denial of consent.

d) The circumstances militate in favor of the validity of the exchange of consent.

Both parties were Catholic, educated in Catholic schools, from religiously observant families. The premarital instruction of the parties was conducted by a priest truly expert in pastoral practice, who was strictly observing the canonical regulations.

The marriage lasted several years and was blessed with the birth of several children.

Therefore, the will of the woman respondent to marry is quite clear; thus whether the case is examined under the species of convalidation, or, and this is more correct, judged under the species of total simulation, there is no proof of a defect of consent, because Juliana intended to give herself to the man as his wife in the celebration before the Church, and because she considered herself united to the man already at the time of their civil marriage, such an intention should be considered as an implicit consent, and in fact actual, to enter into the marriage before the Church.

Having explained everything both in law and in fact, We, the undersigned Auditors of the *Turnus*, sitting for the Tribunal and having only God before our eyes, having invoked the name of Christ, decide, declare and definitively sentence responding to the proposed doubt:

> NEGATIVELY, THAT IS, THERE IS NO PROOF OF NULLITY OF MARRIAGE IN THE CASE ON THE GROUNDS OF DEFECT OF CONVALIDATION OF THE MATRIMONIAL CONSENT ON THE PART OF THE WOMAN RESPONDENT.

Thus we pronounce and also commit to the local Ordinaries and administrators of the Tribunal, to whom it pertains, that they communicate this Our definitive sentence to all parties, who have interest in this case, with respect to all effects of law.

Given in Rome, at the seat of the Tribunal of the Roman Rota on 19 July 2007.

Kenneth E. BOCCAFOLA
Iordanus CABERLETTI
Abdou YAACOUB, *Ponens*

What follows is the text of the December 17, 2007 letter by the Signatura to a number of Bishops, upon review of cases decided under the heading of Invalid Convalidation.

SUPREMO TRIBUNALE DELLA
SEGNATURA APOSTOLICA
Prot. N. 1034/07 SAT
185/07 ES
Defective convalidation
19th December 2007

Your Eminence

The Supreme Tribunal of the Apostolic Signatura has the task of promoting the correct administration 1of justice in the Church, of exercising oversight over the same (cf. artt. 121 and 124, n. 1 Ap. Const. *Pastor bonus)*, and of safeguarding a correct jurisprudence (cf. art. 17, §1 of its Special Norms).

After studying some decrees issued by the Court of Appeals, Province of Chicago, and a sentence issued at first instance by the Metropolitan Tribunal of the Archdiocese of Chicago, on the ground of *defective convalidation*, this Apostolic Signatura considers it advisable to offer some clarifications that will enable both Tribunals to check the correctness of their jurisprudence and to judge such cases without error.

1. In these cases one must keep in mind the *presumptions iuris* which govern every marriage, namely:
   - a marriage is presumed to be valid until the contrary is proven (cf. can. 1060);
   - the internal consent is presumed to be in conformity with the signs or words used in the celebration of the marriage (cf. can. 1101, §1).

   The application of these presumptions to a marriage celebrated in the canonical form lead to some conclusions:
   - the consent expressed according to the canonical form must be presumed valid, until the contrary is proven;
   - the proof of a defect of consent in view of a declaration of the nullity of marriage must therefore follow the usual criteria, taking into account the established Rotal jurisprudence that has developed secure models of proof regarding defects or flaws of consent.
2. Can. 1160 refers to the convalidation of a marriage contracted invalidly because of a defect in the canonical form. The prevailing doctrine does not consider said canon to regard also an attempted civil marriage or one attempted in a non-Catholic rite, in those cases in which at least one party was bound to the canonical form. In fact, no judicial process is required for the declaration of nullity of such an attempted marriage. In any event, one must remember that in such a case a celebration in the canonical form is required.
3. The requirement of can. 1157 refers clearly to the convalidation of a marriage which is invalid because of a diriment impediment (cf. can. 1156, §1) and not to the convalidation of a marriage which is null because of a defect in the canonical form.

   At times it is claimed that from the psychological point of view there cannot be a matrimonial consent when one does not know or at least suppose that the attempted marriage was null. In this regard, it is important to keep-in mind that:

- psychologically it is sufficient to have a vague understanding that the attempted civil marriage or the one attempted in a non-Catholic rite lacked some element which the Catholic Church considers significant;
- this sufficient understanding does not require that the parties know how to explain it in a technical-canonical manner, nor does this sufficient understanding exclude the possibility that on the emotional level the parties continue to attribute some value (e.g. existential or in civil law) to the preceding union, for example, by celebrating its anniversary;
- nor is it required that the parties be able to explain in a technical-canonical manner what happened in the celebration of the marriage in the canonical form; even when they use certain non-technical expressions such as "blessing" to describe it, one must presume, until the contrary has been proven, that in the celebration in the canonical form consent was duly expressed and given;
- even when a party considered the celebration of the marriage in the canonical form to have no value, can. 1100 should be considered: "The knowledge or opinion of the nullity of a marriage does not necessarily exclude matrimonial consent."

Your Eminence is kindly asked to share this letter with the Judges, the Defenders of the Bond, the Promoter of Justice and Advocates who work at the Court of Appeals, Province of Chicago and at the Metropolitan Tribunal of the Archdiocese of Chicago, and to see that both Tribunals follow these directives in handling such cases.

Taking the occasion to express to Your Eminence my sentiments of respect and esteem, I remain

Devotedly Yours,
Agostino Cardinal VALLINI, *Prefect*
Velasio DE PAOLIS, C.S., *Secretary*

Canon 1364

DECLARATION OF EXCOMMUNICATION FOR SCHISM AND HERESY CONGREGATION FOR THE DOCTRINE OF THE FAITH

On July 1, 2007, the Congregation for the Doctrine of the Faith issued a declaration of excommunication concerning the movement called "Community of the Lady of All Nations" and its satellite "Army of Mary."

The CDF declared that the Rev Jean-Pierre Mastropietro attempted diaconal and presbyteral ordinations of six men. These were declared invalid. He, those men who took part in the attempted ordinations, and those who continue to be associated with it, have *ipso facto* incurred excommunication *latae sententiae* due to schism.

Also, the leader/foundress of the sect apparently preached that she herself was the reincarnation of the Blessed Virgin Mary, Mother of God. She has been consequently declared excommunicated *latae sententiae* for heresy.

The CDF also issued an advisory that those who "knowingly" and "deliberately" embrace the same doctrine are excommunicated *latae sententiae* due to the commission of the same heresy.

For online references, see Canadian Conference of Catholic Bishops, Sept 14, 2007 (Quebec City) or Google (AFP) "Army of Mary" (Sept 2007)

Canon 1378

ATTEMPTED ORDINATION OF WOMAN

L'Osservatore Romano daily issue of May 30, 2008, page 1:
[Unofficial translation]

Congregation for the Doctrine of the Faith

General Decree

Regarding the crime of attempting sacred ordination of a woman

The Congregation for the Doctrine of the Faith, to protect the nature and validity of the sacrament of holy orders, in virtue of the special faculty conferred to it by the supreme authority of the Church (see canon 30 of the *Code of Canon Law*), in the Ordinary Session of December 19, 2007, has decreed:

With due regard for what has been established by canon 1378 of the *Code of Canon Law*, both he who has attempted to confer holy orders on a woman, and the woman who has attempted to receive the said sacrament, incurs a *latae sententiae* excommunication, reserved to the Apostolic See.

If he who has attempted to confer holy orders on a woman or if the woman who has attempted to receive holy orders is a member of the faithful subject to the *Code of Canons of the Eastern Churches*, with due regard for what has been established by canon 1443 of the same *Code*, they will be punished with major excommunication, whose remission remains reserved to the Apostolic See (see canon 1423, *Code of Canons of the Eastern Churches*).

The current decree will come into immediate force from the moment of publication in the *L'Osservatore Romano* and is absolute and universal.

William Cardinal Levada, Prefect
Angelo Amato, S.D.B.
Titular Archbishop of Sila, Secretary

CANON 1620 ET AL.: COMPLAINT OF NULLITY AND CANON 1628 ET AL.

NULLITY OF MARRIAGE:
AN APPEAL AGAINST NEGATIVE SENTENCE IN FIRST INSTANCE;
A COMPLAINT OF NULLITY AGAINST FIRST INSTANCE;
A COMPLAINT OF NULLITY AGAINST
THE APPEAL COURT'S INTERLOCUTORY SENTENCE;
AND THE ROTA'S TWO DECISIONS:
NULLITY OF APPEAL COURT SENTENCE
AND OTHER APPEALS REFERRED BACK
TO SECOND INSTANCE COURT

This case is interesting because of the number of procedural issues it raises: a negative decision in First Instance; an appeal against that decision and a complaint of nullity against that decision; an interlocutory sentence by the Second Instance court, and an appeal against that decision by Respondent's First Instance advocate.

At several points the Rota underscores procedural issues that the case raises, and the two questions to be decided by decree: the nullity of the Appeal Court's interlocutory sentence and whether or not to recommend the case to the Rota.

I am grateful to Msgr. Fred Easton for translating the case, and the ponens who made it available. I have made all identifying specifics anonymous.

Prot. N. 2007

DECREE OF THE TURNUS

The undersigned Fathers and Auditors of the Turnus, legitimately called together at this Apostolic Tribunal (date) have issued this decree to decide the following questions:

1) Whether the Interlocutory Sentence - issued by the Appeal Tribunal of the Large Diocese in the U.S. in 2005 which declared null the sentence of first instance which was issued in 2004 by the Tribunal of the Other Diocese in America - is itself null and void?

2) Whether the Turnus should recommend that His Excellency the Dean call the case to be heard before the Roman Rota.

Species facti:

1. Mr. Smith, the petitioner in the case, presented a libellus to the Tribunal of Other Diocese in June 2003 requesting the declaration of nullity of his marriage which he had celebrated with Miss Jones, the respondent, in January 1968 in the Church of St. Therese in Other Diocese.

The called upon tribunal concorded the doubt in 2003 according to the following formula: "The plaintiff did not appear to have the level of discretion required for marriage as it is required for its recognition of ecclesiastical validity by the Roman Catholic Church in its understanding and interpretation of marriage."

When the instruction of the case, conducted mostly through written responses to questions was completed, the Tribunal of Other Diocese Tribunal in 2004 issued a negative sentence, declaring that the nullity of the marriage in the case had not been proven on the grounds of grave lack of discretion of judgment on the part of the petitioner.

2. A Rotal advocate, Mr. Allen, was then constituted as the petitioner's Advocate by his mandate given on ... 2004; this new lawyer then introduced an appeal against the first instance sentence to the Tribunal of Appeal of Large Diocese. Next the lawyer properly pursued his appeal, however, joining to it also a *complaint of nullity* of the sentence itself.

3. The judicial vicar of the Tribunal of Appeal then, in a rather informal manner (i.e. without a prior decree of the Constitution of the Tribunal determining in detail the judges competent to decide the appeal and querela), in early 2005 asked the petitioner's lawyer for further reasons to support his claim of the nullity of the sentence. After the arguments in favor of the nullity of the sentence were provided by the petitioner's lawyer, the Tribunal of Appeal, *mirabile dictu*!, immediately — i.e., without taking care to notify the other party that a complaint of nullity of sentence had been made, and moreover, entirely neglecting the citation of the other parties for the handling of the incidental question , i. e. the Defender of the Bond and the Promoter of Justice, in mid 2005 hastily and rashly issued an Interlocutory Sentence by which it declared that the nullity of the sentence issued by the Other Diocese in 2004 was evident.

4. When the Interlocutory Sentence of the Tribunal of Appeal was then published, the Defender of the Bond of first instance, completely forgetting both that his competence with regard to this case was completely exhausted once the decision of First Instance was rendered and that this matter would now pertain to the Defender of the Bond of Second Instance who was the one who enjoyed the right of appeal against a decision of a tribunal of Second Instance, expressed his will that there be an appeal against this interlocutory decision to the Roman Rota.

After having received notice for the first time, and only after the publication of the Interlocutory Sentence, of the complaint of nullity of the First Instance sentence, the Reverend Advocate for the respondent, a few days afterwards, in his own letter of appeal with regard to the merits of the Interlocutory Sentence, made his own new complaint of nullity against the actual Interlocutory Sentence of mid-2004, claiming that the right of defense relative to the incidental decision was denied to the respondent.

5. Once the Rotal Turnus was constituted, the undersigned Ponens, having considered the *votum* of the Defender of the Bond, Rev. Father Stevens, and having provided for an *ex officio* advocate for the respondent, in early 2007 established, in accord with Canon 1589, that the questions would be resolved by decree and that the parties in the case were to prepare their respective arguments. Then, having received the briefs of the Advocate for the petitioner, Mr. Smith, of the *ex officio* Advocate of the Respondent, Mr. Place, and of the Promoter of Justice, Reverend Father, the undersigned Auditors have today come together in accord with the law to respond to the following questions:

1. Is the Interlocutory Sentence of the Tribunal of Appeal of the Large Diocese in the United States issued in early 2005 which declared null the Sentence of Other Diocese in mid-2004, itself null and void?
2. Whether the Turnus should recommend to his Excellency the Dean, that he call the case to be heard before the Roman Rota?

6. The principal reason for declaring the nullity of the Interlocutory Sentence issued in this case by the tribunal of appeal is set forth in the jurisprudence of Our Forum in a case from Melbourne in 2006 before the undersigned *Ponens*:

"... violations have occurred in the very process used for deciding a complaint of nullity of sentence. For... we note the absence of any intervention by the Promoter of Justice throughout the entire process... Since the validity of a judicial sentence is a question which clearly pertains to the public good, most certainly the Promoter of Justice is to be heard in deciding the precise incidental question concerning the validity of a sentence. Moreover, Canon 1433 of the Code of Canon Law establishes that in cases in which the presence of the Promoter of Justice or Defender of the Bond is required, if they are not cited, the acts are null. And, in this case, that is, regarding the question of a complaint of nullity of sentence, the acts demonstrate that certainly there was no citation of, nor actual intervention by the Promoter of Justice [of the tribunal of appeal]."

There can be no doubt, therefore, that for this reason the Interlocutory Sentence itself, according to Canon 1433, was infected with nullity and, therefore, was void and invalid and cannot be confirmed.

7. Furthermore, from the acts of the case it is also clear that the Respondent was in no way notified, and certainly not cited, for the purposes of responding to the incidental question; the respondent had no knowledge that this question was being handled. Therefore, according to Canon 1511: "If the citation was not communicated legitimately, the acts of the process are null..."

It is true that the Tribunal of Appeal in one act of notification to the Respondent in late 2004 communicated the following: "I wish to inform you that in October, 2004, the negative decision which was rendered in the above named case was appealed to the appellate court by the plaintiff, Mr. Smith [*Summarium*, page 26]." But, absolutely nothing was said about the complaint of nullity of the sentence, even though earlier in October the lawyer for the petitioner had already, in fact, brought the complaint of nullity of sentence.

For this reason, the Respondent and her proper Advocate were *de facto* unable to exercise their right of defense, that is, to sustain the validity of the Sentence of First Instance of Other Diocese. The Tribunal of Appeal did not permit the Respondent to have the faculty of defending her position, of replying or of being heard.

Only after the fact, that is, after the publication of the Interlocutory Sentence, was the lawyer for the Respondent able to observe: "The Interlocutory Sentence violates the Respondent's right of defense, violating the letter and spirit of Canon 50 in the Code of Canon Law."

Clearly, there is manifest nullity of the Interlocutory Sentence because of the denial of the right of defense both to the Respondent and to the Promoter of Justice according to Canon 1620, 7°.

8. We entirely pass over a discussion of the question of the invalid mandate by which the Petitioner, Mr. Smith appointed his own advocate, Mr. Allen, which was first drawn up and implemented at a time after the sentence of first instance was published. Thus it could have had no invalidating effect on the judgment and process of first instance, which had already been concluded by the issuance

of the definitive sentence. In any case, however, Advocate Allen has presented to Our Apostolic Tribunal a new and valid mandate correctly authenticated by the signature of the notary.

Moreover, the lawyer of the Respondent, Mr. Place, makes a wise observation regarding the incongruities in the reasoning process of the judges of the Tribunal of Appeal. For they first declare: "It is decreed that, at this time, Mr. Allen does not have a valid mandate to function as Procurator and Advocate for the Petitioner. As such, he does not have standing to submit either an appeal or complaint of nullity against the definitive sentence issued by the Tribunal of the Other Diocese in mid- 2004 *[Summarium*, page 37]."

But, then, in fact, the Tribunal of Appeal, *mirabile dictu!* declared the nullity of the sentence as requested by the very same Advocate!

It did this, notwithstanding the fact that since Advocate Allen was not a legitimate Procurator and Advocate of the Petitioner he consequently was not able to pursue the action nor, even less so, to introduce a new juridic action, namely, a complaint of nullity of sentence. As a consequence, the Interlocutory Sentence which was issued is contrary to Canon 1501 and, according to Canon 1620, 4°, is invalid.

9. Concerning the observation made by the Defender of the Bond of this Our Apostolic Tribunal, Rev. Father Stevens, namely, that there is no appeal allowed against the interlocutory sentence (Canon 1629, 4°), we respond that in this case the impugned interlocutory sentence in reality has the effect of a definitive sentence, because, according to Canon 1618, it imposes an end to the trial, by canceling out the first instance.

The Promoter of Justice in this case, Msgr. Murson, agrees with this and in his amended *votum* notes: "From a comparison of Canon 1618 and 1629, 4°, the woman Respondent has the right to appeal against the decision reached by the Interlocutory Sentence, which declared null the negative sentence of first instance, since the aforementioned decision had the force of a definitive sentence, from the very fact that it put an end to the first level of judgment. Therefore, the aforementioned interlocutory sentence is able to be appealed."

Together with his appeal to the Rota the lawyer for the Respondent also included a complaint about the nullity of the Interlocutory Sentence itself: "On the Respondent's behalf, I am proposing a complaint of nullity against this interlocutory sentence [page 40]." And therefore, we respond in our decision to this precise question.

10. With regard to the second question, namely, whether the case should be called to the Roman Rota at the second degree of jurisdiction, we note that the case was specifically appealed by the Petitioner to the ordinary Tribunal of Appeal which, as a result, took the case into its own hands. A sentence on the merits at the second degree of jurisdiction has not yet been issued by the natural Tribunal of Appeal, and so, consequently, the undersigned Prelate Auditors determine that the case is to be remitted to the Tribunal of Large Diocese, where the parties can exercise their rights.

Having set forth above all matters both the law and in fact and having assiduously examined them, the undersigned Auditors of the Turnus, taking into account the briefs of the Patron [lawyer] of the Petitioner, Advocate Allen and the Patron [lawyer] of the Respondent, Advocate Place, together with the animadversions of the Promoter of Justice of this Apostolic Tribunal, Msgr. Murson, as well as the Defender of the Bond, Rev. Father Stevens, thus respond to the questions which have been posed:

> I. **AFFIRMATIVE**, that is, the nullity of the interlocutory sentence issued by the tribunal of appeal in 2005 has been established.
>
> II. **NEGATIVE**, that is, the calling of the case before the roman rota is not to be recommended.

This decree is to be communicated to all concerned, for the purpose of achieving all the effects of law.

Given at Rome, at the seat of the Tribunal the Roman Rota, June, 2007.

Turnus

CANONS 1255 – OWNERSHIP OF PROPERTY
CANONS 1405, 1406 – COMPETENCE OF HOLY SEE
CANON 1419: ABSOLUTE INCOMPETENCE OF OTHER TRIBUNALS

This case is interesting for several reasons: it involves a question of ownership of property in Australia, a complaint of nullity of sentence, and the question of which tribunal has competence to hear such cases against a bishop or a diocese. The Rota's decree was sent to the CLSA for publication in Roman Replies by the ponens Monsignor Kenneth E. Boccafola. The specifics have been altered.

Coram R. P. D. KENNETH E. BOCCAFOLA
MELBURNEN.
Iuris Proprietatis: Incid. Null. Sent.
Seamans Association of City vs. The Archdiocese

P.N. ==
DECREE

The undersigned Prelate Auditors, namely Mons. Kenneth E. BOCCAFOLA, the Ponens, and Mons. Pius Vitus PINTO, and Mons. Gerard McKAY, met at the Tribunal of the Roman Rota on 22 June 2006 to decide whether to confirm or overturn the Decree of the National Appeal Tribunal of [country] of [date] 2004 which declared that the Sentence of first instance issued by that same Tribunal in this case on [date] 2004 was not null.

SUMMARY OF THE CASE:

1. The principal object of controversy in this case is the right of ownership of a piece of property at "Small Street" in the city of [...], State of [...], [country]. For on [date] 2003 Mr. Mahon, President of the Association which goes by the generic name of "Seamans Association" which was civilly incorporated under the title of "Seamans Inc." presented a libellus to the National Appeal Tribunal of [country] asking that it be declared the rightful owner of the aforesaid property since it felt that it had obtained ownership by prescription in accord with canons 1268, 197-199 and 1270.

2. It seems useful first of all to briefly summarize the facts.

Providing for the pastoral care of seafarers was an important need in the port of [city] in the 19th and 20th centuries because of the significant maritime commerce of the city. At first the needs of the seafarers were met by private initiatives of the faithful, and particularly those promoted by the St. Vincent de Paul Conference. Gradually the hierarchical authorities recognized their competence, and at the urging of the Holy See, confided the task to the Apostolate of the Sea.

In the port of [city] the aforesaid pastoral ministry, with the approval of successive Archbishops, was exercised by a local Association constituted according to the norms of the Holy See, that is under the leadership of the Port Chaplain. At the beginning the use of a building at Small Street on a property within the confines of the Cathedral Parish, was granted to the Port Chaplain and his fellow workers as the seat of their association. Later on the Cathedral parish was divided and the new Parish of St. Ambrose, in whose territory the aforesaid property was now located, was erected. In 1968, the Port Chaplain was also named the Pastor of the Parish of St. Ambrose.

In the State of [State] and in [country] the Catholic Church as such lacks juridical personality in the civil law; thus a civil juridic entity named "*The Roman Catholic Trusts Corporation for the Diocese of [city]*" was established and recognized by the State of [state] in order for the Church to exercise its rights of ownership. As its very title (in the plural, "Trusts") suggests, several canonical entities exercise their rights of ownership in a civilly valid way under its aegis.

The Archbishop of [city] in [date] allowed the Association indefinite use of the aforesaid property (the property which was first a portion of the territory of the Cathedral Parish and then a portion located within the territory of St. Ambrose), which use was to be a partial economic aid for the work of the Apostolate, which was also funded in part by a special collection (can. 1266 CIC and can. 1508 CIC/17) and also by the initiatives and generosity of the members of the aforesaid association.

In time, circumstances changed for the Apostleship of the Sea, for the parish of St. Ambrose and for the Archdiocese of [city] itself so that eventually a change in the use of the property was proposed, which change would have significantly restricted the freedom of administration heretofore enjoyed by the Association. Hence arose the controversy over the right of ownership of the property which was then submitted to the ecclesiastical Tribunal.

3. The Judicial Vicar of the Tribunal approached constituted a one judge court on [date] 2003; the libellus, presented in accord with can. 1419, §2 CIC, but not taking into account can. 1405, §3, n. 3, was accepted on 24 July 2003 and the parties were cited for the concordance of the doubt.

The Respondent proposed a counter suit on [date] 2003 seeking a declaration that the Apostleship of the Sea was distinct from the Association; at the same time the Archdiocese also raised the question of the incompetence of the Appeal Tribunal of [country] based on can. 1405, §3, n. 1 and n. 3..

The Judge, after having heard the parties but without any input from the Promoter of Justice, declared on [date] 2003 that his Court was competent. In the same decree he also established that the question to be decided was the following: "... the point at issue is the ownership of the property at Small Street [city]." No official notice was taken of the countersuit.

4. The case was instructed by gathering together relevant documentation, but no actual witness was cited or heard even though each side had proposed a list of witnesses. Next, by his decree of [date] 2004 the Judicial Vicar of the Appeal Tribunal of [country], without a special mandate of the Episcopal Moderator of the Tribunal (can. 1425, §2), increased the number of Judges, thereby constituting a Collegiate Tribunal of three Judges. The Acts of the case were published and a decree of conclusion of the case was issued. Thus the Tribunal on [date] 2004 issued its sentence of first instance which decided that the Association had not proven its ownership of the property.

5. On [date] 2004 the Judicial Vicar of the Appeal Tribunal of [country] notified the parties of the definitive sentence. On [date] 2004 Mr. Mahon on behalf of the Association interposed a complaint of nullity of the sentence. The Appeal Tribunal, taking into account the observations and remarks of the petitioner and also of the respondent and their lawyers, but without citing or receiving any input from the Promoter of Justice, on [date] 2004 rejected the complaint of nullity of its sentence. Thus on [date] 2005 - within the term of thirty days granted by the judges of first instance - the Association appealed both the decision concerning the rejected complaint of nullity and the decision concerning the merit of the case to our Tribunal of the Roman Rota.

The Turnus of Judges was then constituted and Rotal Advocates were nominated to defend the rights of the parties. The Ponens then determined that the incidental question would be decided by decree, after hearing the arguments of the parties and the opinion of the Promoter of Justice. Thus today the undersigned Prelate Auditors are gathered together to decide the following question: "Shall the Decree of the Appeal Tribunal of [country] of [date] 2004 which rejected the nullity of the first instance sentence issued on [date] 2004 by the same Tribunal about the ownership of property be confirmed or overturned?"

In Iure and In Facto

6. The undersigned Rotal Judges respond to the above question as follows: the decision which rejected the complaint of nullity of the sentence must be overturned for several reasons, but principally because the Appeal Judges did not rightly interpret the meaning of can. 1419, §2 and neglected can. 1405, §3, n.1 and n. 3. Accordingly, the National Appeal Tribunal of [country] was absolutely incompetent to handle the case and therefore their sentence of [date] 2004 was null and void.

Concerning the Absolute Incompetence of the National Appeal Tribunal of [country].

7. The norms to determine the competent forum are given in cann. 1404-1416 CIC. Specifically in this case it is necessary to accurately distinguish between the competence mentioned in can. 1405 §3 CIC and that mentioned in can. 1419, §2. The two competences spoken of are not redundant nor are they identical with one another.

For can. 1405, §3, n. 1 applies in the case of anyone who has the episcopal character. Because of the dignity of the person of a Bishop anyone who wishes to bring a case directly against any Bishop must bring the case, even if it is in the first instance, only before the Roman Rota. The canon specifically says: "It is reserved to the Roman Rota to judge Bishops in contentious cases ...".

For a similar reason anyone who wishes to bring into Court not the Bishop himself, but the Diocese - whose legitimate representative is of course the Diocesan Bishop - must according to can. 1405 §3, n. 3 bring the case before this Apostolic Forum. For again the canon specifically states: "It is reserved to the Roman Rota to judge dioceses ... ". Contentious cases of dioceses are therefore always reserved to our apostolic forum. And the reason is clear: only the Roman Pontiff in the Latin Church (cf. can. 1062, §3 CCEO) is Judge and Superior of the particular churches: and it is in his name and with his authority that the Tribunal of the Roman Rota, whose members by their office share the ordinary vicarious judicial power of the Pontiff, administer justice in this type of case.

The competence of the Roman Rota in these cases is exclusive as mentioned in can. 1406 §2 CIC. Therefore a sentence issued in such a case by any other judge will be insanably null according to the norm of can. 1620, n. 1 because of his absolute incompetence.

8. On the other hand can. 1419 CIC refers to another type of situation. For, besides the case of the Diocese, a case which is specifically regulated by can. 1405 §3, n. 3, the Bishop can likewise represent (can. 1480, §2) other juridical persons which exist in the diocese and which have the Diocesan Bishop as their Superior, as for example the Diocesan Seminary or a Catholic school, or a Catholic hospital. In this case the competent forum in first instance is no longer the Diocesan tribunal (in which the Diocesan Bishop is the natural judge, and therefore it is not suitable for him to be, as it were, a judge in his own case) but rather the Bishop's ordinary Tribunal of Appeal.

If any doubt should still remain about this interpretation it suffices to consult the work of the Commission for the Revision of the Code. The Fathers of that Commission specifically added the word "dioceses" to the text of canon 1405 precisely to avoid errors of interpretation which might arise. Nor can the exclusive competence of the Roman Rota in the case of Dioceses be called in doubt (cf. *Communicationes* 10 [1978], p. 221; cf. Z. Grocholewski, *Comentario Exegetico, sub canone 1419*, IV/1, Pamplona 1995, p. 770: "En todo caso, juzgar a la diocesis ... esta reservado a la Rota Romana").

Concerning the Parties' Legal Standing:

9. Another serious reason for overturning the Decree of [date] 2004 is that the appealed judges neglected to deal with ["... prescinding from the question of the juridical existence of the petitioner", p. 317] a preliminary question of the greatest importance. They left unanswered a matter that greatly affects the outcome of the case and impacts on the very validity of the sentence which was about to be issued. And it is the question of who are the actual parties in the case: the judges must necessarily determine the legal right of each party to stand in judgment.

For in the Church there exist either physical persons or juridic persons (can. 113, §2 CIC). Juridic persons are established to pursue ends congruent to the mission of the Church which surpass the capacities of single individual persons. A person, whether physical or juridic, is the subject of rights and obligations. Among the rights of persons is the right of patrimony, that is, of acquiring, retaining, administering and disposing of temporal goods (can. 1255).

A juridic person in the Church is constituted either by the law itself - e. g. the Holy See, a diocese, a parish, a diocesan seminary, etc. - or by concession of the competent authority given by written decree (cann. 114, §1, 116 §2; cf. 299 §3). The juridic person of the Diocese, according to can. 393, is administered by the Diocesan Bishop and is represented by him in all of its dealings. The juridic person of the parish is likewise, according to can. 523, administered only by the pastor.

10. In this case one can make a good argument that the Association has no canonical juridic personality. For the Association obtained juridic personality according to the civil law only in the last few years and did so contrary to the will of the Archbishop. Everyone admits that there is no decree by competent ecclesiastical authority conferring canonical juridic personality on this association. Hence, the group of physical persons who make up the Association, since they never were granted canonical juridic personality, must be considered simply as a series of different individual physical persons. No one of these in his own right as an individual is asserting that he owns the disputed property, nor does anyone in his own name claim possession and use of the disputed property.

It seems therefore that the Association, lacking juridic personality, has no right to stand in judgment as a Petitioner. In fact the Pontifical Commission for the Interpretation of Legislative Texts has denied, in a similar case, that a group of the faithful as such, has such a right [Cf. *Responsio diei 12 decembris 1988* in E. Caparros, ed. *Code of Canon Law Annotated*, Montreal 1993, p. 1286].

Thus there exists a further reason for declaring the nullity of the sentence of first instance of [date] 2004, since the decision was given for parties, at least one of whom did not have the right to stand before the court (can. 1620, n. 5). Certainly also for this reason then we must overturn the Decree of [date] 2004 of the National Appeal Tribunal of [country].

11. Furthermore, it might perhaps be true that the other party, the Archdiocese of [city], in this particular case, also did not have legal standing to be the Respondent cited in the trial concluded by the impugned sentence.

For we have seen above that it is only according to the civil law, that is, under "*The Roman Catholic Trusts Corporation for the Diocese of Melbourne*", but not under canon law, that the Archdiocese is invested with the ownership of properties belonging to diverse ecclesiastical entities such as parishes, etc.

But juridic persons in the Church stand before the court by means of their legitimate representatives (can. 1480, §1). Specifically the diocese stands before the court through its Bishop and the parish only through its pastor. Whenever a juridic person is erroneously represented in court by someone other than the proper person designated according to can. 1279, §1 it would seem that a definitive sentence in such a case would suffer from insanable nullity in accord with the norm of c. 1620, n. 5.

Since this is so, an important preliminary question, that is, who would be the true legitimate representative capable of standing in judgement in canon law concerning the right of ownership of the property at Small Street, [city], i. e. , whether it would be the Archbishop of [city] or the Pastor of St. Ambrose Parish, would necessarily have had to have been determined at the beginning of the trial in order to avoid the danger of issuing a null sentence.

Furthermore, if the juridic person cited should have actually been the Parish of St. Ambrose to be represented by its Pastor, then in that case the Appeal Tribunal of [country] should not have been used, but rather the ordinary Diocesan Tribunal of first instance. And so also for this additional reason the impugned sentence would have to be judged insanably null based on c. 1440 compared with can. 1620 §1.

12. Finally, the Decree of [date] 2004 must be overturned due to the violations of law which took place in the very process for deciding the complaint of nullity of the sentence, and which have been pointed out by our Promoter of Justice. For we have already noted the absence of any input of the Promoter of Justice of the Appeal Tribunal during the entire process in which the competence of that Tribunal was challenged and decided.

Since the validity of a judicial sentence is a matter which clearly concerns the public good, certainly the Promoter of Justice should have been heard in the precise incidental question concerning the invalidity of this sentence. Furthermore, c. 1433 in fact prescribes that in cases in which the presence of the promoter of justice or the defender of the bond is required, if they should not be cited to take part, the acts of that case are null. And in the case concerning the complaint of nullity, the acts show that there was no citation of nor actual input of the Promoter of Justice.

There is no doubt that for these reasons the Decree [date, 2004] which denied *[n.b. material error in original, which has "declarata"]* the nullity of the sentence cannot be confirmed. Rather there exist several serious arguments to fully uphold the nullity of the original sentence, with which arguments the undersigned Auditors fully agree.

13. Thus by this present Decree the Decree of the National Appeal Tribunal of [country] of [date] 2004 is overturned. It follows then that the sentence issued by the same Tribunal on [date] 2004 is null. And, since there is no appeal from a sentence vitiated by nullity, the case is sent back to the Curia of [Archdiocese].

Nonetheless, in accord with c. 1446 §2 the parties should be encouraged to come to a mutual agreement in order to settle the question in an equitable manner. And, mindful of the tenor of c. 1715 §1, it might take place through ecclesiastical judicial arbitration [cf. cann. 1713-1716] in order that more serious damage to the public good of the Church may not possibly occur from the prosecution of the case in the civil forum.

In any case, if the attempt to peacefully resolve the dispute should have no result, those whom it actually concerns may still exercise their right, taking into account, however, the proper juridic person, whether of the Archdiocese, the Archbishop or other.

Therefore, having considered all of the above *in iure et in facto*, the undersigned Prelate Auditors of the Turnus, having considered the acts of the case and the sentence, and having weighed the arguments of the Advocate of the Petitioner, Adv. Dominic Teti, and the Adv. of the Respondent, Martha Wegan, along with the opinion of the Promoter of Justice, Rev. Sebastian Paciolla, hereby respond to the proposed question:

In the negative, that is, the Decree of [date] 2004 is overturned and therefore the Sentence of [date] 2004 is declared null. The case is returned to the Curia of [Archdiocese], so that those whom it concerns may exercise their right.

This Decree is to be notified to all whom it concerns for all legal effects. The judicial expenses are determined to be Euro 1000.00 and are to be divided equally between the parties.

Given at the Tribunal of the Roman Rota on 22 June 2006
Kenneth E. BOCCAFOLA, Ponens
Pius Vito PINTO
Gerardus McKAY

Advisory Opinions

Introductory Note

The following opinions were developed in response to inquiries received by the CLSA Committee on Advisory Opinions or assembled by the Committee from among those submitted to the Society for publication. The opinions carry only the weight of the persons named at the end of each opinion. They do not represent the opinion of the diocese or institution with which the author is affiliated. Advisory opinions are not authentic interpretations of the law, but reflect the scholarly and practical insights of the contributors.

For the convenience of our readers, the opinions are arranged according to the canons of the *Code of Canon Law* and the *Code of Canons of the Eastern Churches*. The original questions have been abbreviated or summarized, and the opinions edited to protect the anonymity of the inquirer or to conform to the style of CLSA publications.

The Committee expresses profound gratitude to the canonists who participated in this year's publication. The continued success of this annual project is a result of their willingness to share their time and talent in service to this important work.The Committee is interested in receiving opinions that members have formulated in response to specific inquiries and inquiries in need of responses. The Committee also welcomes the participation of members who wish to be involved in this annual project by offering to render opinions to inquiries received by the Committee.

Inquiries or contributions to *CLSA Advisory Opinions* may be directed to the undersigned editor at:

United States Conference of Catholic Bishops
Secretariat of Doctrine
3211 Fourth Street, N.E.
Washington, DC 20017-1194
(202) 541-3016
E-mail: sverbeek@usccb.org

Ms. Siobhan M. Verbeek, J.C.L. Editor
Rev. Msgr. Ronny E. Jenkins, J.C.D., Associate Editor
Ms. Jaclyn O'Brien McEachern, J.C.L., Associate Editor
Dr. Lynda A. Robitaille, J.C.D., Associate Editor

Canon 230

USE OF FEMALE ALTAR SERVERS IN LITURGICAL CELEBRATIONS USING THE EXTRAORDINARY FORM

Our diocese recently promulgated norms for the implementation of the apostolic letter, Summorum Pontificum, *concerning the extraordinary form of the celebration of the Mass and sacraments. The norms indicate that for liturgical celebrations using the extraordinary form, the function of altar server is reserved to males, whether youth or adults, in accord with the prescripts of the 1962* Roman Missal. *Is it true that females are restricted from fulfilling the function of altar server when celebrating the extraordinary form of the Roman rite?*

OPINION

The prohibition of the use of female altar servers was clearly stated in the 1917 *Code of Canon Law* (c. 813, §2). The October 1, 1949, instruction of the Sacred Congregation for the Discipline of the Sacraments, *Quam plurimum,* warned that "all the authors teach unanimously that it is forbidden under pain of mortal sin for women, even nuns, to serve *at the altar.*"[1] Presumably, these are the "prescripts" to which the diocesan norms refer to justify the continued prohibition of female altar servers when celebrating what *Summorum Pontificum* calls "the extraordinary form" of the Roman rite.[2]

It should be noted that the above-mentioned prohibitions are disciplinary laws which concern the celebration of the Mass. These disciplinary liturgical laws must be kept distinct from the rubrics of the 1962 *Roman Missal,* which are contained within the liturgical rites themselves, and provide directives for the ministers in the celebration of the liturgy.

Numerous new disciplinary laws were promulgated to correspond with the liturgical reforms made in response to the Second Vatican Council's Constitution on the Sacred Liturgy, *Sacrosanctum concilium.* A later law abrogates or derogates from an earlier law when: (1) it expressly states this; (2) it is directly contrary

[1] Sacred Congregation for the Discipline of the Sacraments, Instruction, *Quam plurimum,* "Instruction on Asking Indults for: Private Oratories, Portable Altars: Mass Without a Server: Keeping the Blessed Sacrament in Private Chapels," October 1, 1949, in *Acta Apostolicae Sedis* 41 (1949) 493-511; English translation in *Canon Law Digest* 3:335.

[2] Pope Benedict XVI, Apostolic Letter *motu proprio, Summorum Pontificum,* "On the Use of Pre-conciliar Liturgical Forms," July 7, 2007, in *Acta Apostolicae Sedis* 99 (2007) 777-781; English translation in *Origins* 37 (2007-2008) 129-132.

to the earlier law; or (3) it integrally reorders the whole subject matter of the earlier law (c. 20). Clearly, the flurry of legislative activity following the Second Vatican Council abrogated numerous liturgical disciplinary laws. Many of these new disciplinary laws have since been incorporated into the 1983 *Code of Canon Law*. These new disciplinary laws–the *ius vigens*–govern the entire Roman rite, including both the *forma ordinaria* and the *forma extraordinaria*. The rubrics for each respective form are to be utilized and kept distinct when celebrating either liturgical rite. However, when celebrating the Mass according to the *Roman Missal* of Blessed John XXIII, current disciplinary liturgical laws are binding, and not those which were in place when the Missal was promulgated in 1962.

If the current disciplinary laws govern both the ordinary and extraordinary forms, it is important to determine the current norms concerning the use of female altar servers. Despite significant liturgical changes following the Second Vatican Council, the prohibition of the use of female altar servers was maintained.[3] Since the issue of female altar servers, however, remained a disputed question even after the promulgation of the 1983 Code, the Pontifical Council for the Interpretation of Legislative Texts issued an authentic interpretation in response to a proposed *dubium*. Recall that authentic interpretations have the same force as the law itself (c. 16, § 2). In response to the question whether serving at the altar is reckoned among the roles that lay people, both men and women, may exercise according to canon 230, §2, the Pontifical Council answered in the affirmative, "according to the instruction to be given by the Apostolic See."[4]

This instruction, given in the form of a circular letter issued by the Congregation for Divine Worship and the Discipline of the Sacraments, served to further explain this change in liturgical discipline. The letter notes that while permitting women to serve as altar servers, "it is the competence of each bishop, in his diocese, after hearing the opinion of the episcopal conference, to make a prudential judgment on what to do, with a view to the ordered development of liturgical life

[3] Cf. Sacred Congregation for Divine Worship, Instruction, *Liturgicae instaurationes*, "Third Instruction on the Correct Implementation of the Constitution on the Liturgy," September 5, 1970, in *Acta Apostolicae Sedis* 62 (1970) 692-704; English translation in *Canon Law Digest* 7:40-52; Sacred Congregation for the Sacraments and Divine Worship, *Inaestimabile donum*, "Norms Concerning Worship of the Eucharistic Mystery," April 3, 1980, in *Acta Apostolicae Sedis* 72 (1980) 331-343; English translation in *Canon Law Digest* 9:563-574.

[4] Pontifical Council for the Interpretation of Legislative Texts, Reply, June 6, 1994, in *Acta Apostolicae Sedis* 86 (1994) 541; English translation in *Code of Canon Law Annotated*, 2nd ed., eds. Ernest Caparros and Hélène Aubé (Montréal: Wilson & Lafleur Limitée, 2004), 1621.

in his own diocese."[5] The letter also encourages the preservation of the "noble tradition" of having boys serve at the altar. A similar tone is adopted in the March 25, 2004, instruction of the Congregation for Divine Worship and the Discipline of the Sacraments, *Redemptionis Sacramentum*, no. 47, which extols the practice by which boys provide service at the altar, while also acknowledging that females may be admitted to this ministry, at the discretion of the diocesan bishop.[6]

The decision to use female altar servers remains that of the diocesan bishop, after hearing the opinion of the episcopal conference. John Huels suggests that the circular letter presented four objective criteria for bishops to consider when deciding to admit both males and females to serve at the altar: "(1) the viewpoint of the conference of bishops on this issue, (2) the sensibilities of the faithful, (3) the reasons for using both males and females, and (4) the different liturgical settings and congregations who gather for Mass."[7] If female altar servers are employed in other celebrations of the Mass according to the ordinary form, there is no reason to restrict the use of female altar servers when utilizing the 1962 *Roman Missal* on the basis of abrogated liturgical discipline. Of course, the liturgical setting of the extraordinary form, and the sensibilities of the faithful would be especially important to consider when deciding whether to permit the use of female altar servers when celebrating according to the extraordinary form of the Roman rite. Nevertheless, the same disciplinary laws–the *ius vigens*–govern these two usages of the one Roman rite.

What can be said of the diocesan norms prohibiting the use of female altar servers? The diocesan norms noted above, presumably in the form of an instruction (c. 34, §1), cannot derogate from the law. If there are any provisions contained therein which cannot be reconciled with the provisions of the law, these provisions lack all force (c. 34, §2). While the use of female altar servers is left to the prudential judgment of the diocesan bishop after considering a number of factors noted above, the restriction of such finds no justification in abrogated liturgical discipline.

Chad J. Glendinning, J.C.L.

[5] Congregation for Divine Worship and the Discipline of the Sacraments, Circular Letter, "On the Use of Female Altar Servers," March 15, 1994, in *Notitiae* 30 (1994) 333-335; English translation in *Origins* 23 (1994) 777-779.

[6] Congregation for Divine Worship and the Discipline of the Sacraments, Instruction, *Redemptionis Sacramentum*, "On Certain Matters to be Observed or Avoided Regarding the Eucharist," March 25, 2004, in *Acta Apostolicae Sedis* 96 (2004) 549-601; English translation in *Origins* 33 (2004) 801-822.

[7] John M. Huels, "Can Priests Forbid Girls to Serve Mass?," *Celebrate!*, vol. 41, no. 4 (July-August 2002) 4.

Canons 230 and 915

WITHHOLDING OF HOLY COMMUNION BY EXTRAORDINARY MINISTER

Under what conditions, if any, may extraordinary ministers withhold Holy Communion? (1) My roommate regularly lets her boyfriend spend the night with her in our apartment. I have objected to this behavior, and have been told to mind my own business. If she comes to me for Holy Communion on Sunday, must I give it to her knowing what I do about her conduct?; (2) A prominent, pro-abortion Catholic politician belongs to our parish. I am very uncomfortable giving him Holy Communion. May I withhold it?; (3) A man with an obscene tattoo came to me for Holy Communion. When I saw it, I told him to cover it up. He did, and I gave him Holy Communion. Later, I wondered whether I had any right to say anything, but I also wondered whether I should have given Holy Communion to him knowing what I did about what was under his shirt sleeve. Can you advise?

OPINION

Analysis of these three questions turns primarily on canon 915 of the *Code of Canon Law*: "Those who have been excommunicated or interdicted after the imposition or declaration of the penalty and others obstinately persevering in manifest grave sin are not to be admitted to holy communion." Nothing in this (or any other) canon exempts extraordinary ministers of Holy Communion from the duty incumbent upon all ministers of the Eucharist to protect the Blessed Sacrament from objectively scandalous or sacrilegious reception. Put another way, extraordinary ministers are responsible before ecclesiastical authority, and eventually before God, for their administration of Holy Communion. That said, however, extraordinary ministers are unlikely to know what canonists take for granted, namely, that canon 915, even though it is a sacramental disciplinary norm and not penal law, requires a very careful reading for proper application.[1] We begin with an overview of the rights of the faithful in regard to the reception of the sacraments in general, and the Eucharist in particular.

A complex of canons upholds the faithful's fundamental right to receive the sacraments. Canon 213 asserts the right of the faithful "to receive assistance from the sacred pastors out of the spiritual goods of the Church, especially the word

[1] John M. Huels, Commentary on Canon 915, in *New Commentary on the Code of Canon Law*, eds. John P. Beal, James A. Coriden, and Thomas J. Green (New York, NY: Paulist Press, 2000), 1110-1111.

of God and the sacraments"; canon 843, §1 forbids ministers (including extraordinary ministers) from withholding the sacraments from those "who seek them at appropriate times, are properly disposed, and are not prohibited by law from receiving them"; and canon 912 states that "Any baptized person not prohibited by law can and must be admitted to holy communion." Moreover, canon 18 requires that any law that restricts the exercise of rights (as c. 915 certainly does) be strictly interpreted, that is, that the restrictions be construed as narrowly as reasonably possible. Considered individually or as a group, then, these are strongly pro-reception norms.

Turning to canon 915, and prescinding from the rarely encountered excommunication and interdict situations and from cases wherein a bishop or pastor has made a specific determination, we see that four distinct conditions must be simultaneously satisfied before any minister of Holy Communion, ordinary or extraordinary, may withhold the Eucharist from a member of the faithful; indeed, verification of these four conditions directs withholding of the Eucharist. To occasion withholding the Eucharist under canon 915, the conduct in which a would-be communicant perseveres must be: (1) obstinate, (2) manifest, (3) grave, and (4) sinful. Let's look at these requirements in reverse order.

Sinful. To be "sinful," one's behavior must be objectively contrary to the dictates of faith or morals.[2] Conduct that is offensive, irritating, distasteful, and so on, might or might not be sinful, yet, as the legislative history of canon 915 makes clear, only sinful behavior triggers consequences for reception.[3] Canon 915 does not demand verification that would-be recipients are subjectively guilty for sinful behavior before withholding Holy Communion (canon law hardly expects ministers to read souls), but it does set out that one's conduct must be sinful in the eyes of the Church (not necessarily those of the minister in question) to justify withholding the Eucharist. While extraordinary ministers of Holy Communion are likely to have some sense as to what kinds of behavior are "sinful," they are unlikely to have the background necessary for illuminating factually close cases.

Grave. Having established that conduct must be sinful to render one potentially liable to the withholding of Holy Communion, the conduct in question must be "gravely" sinful.[4] The requirement of "gravity" is an amplification of the requirement of "sinfulness" that serves to underscore that one's behavior must be

[2] *Catechism of the Catholic Church*, 2nd ed. (Washington, DC: Libreria Editrice Vaticana-United States Conference of Catholic Bishops, 2000), nos. 1849-1853.

[3] Edward N. Peters, *Incrementa in Progressu 1983 Codicis Iuris Canonici: A Legislative History of the Code of Canon Law* (Montréal: Wilson & Lafleur, 2005), 837.

[4] *Catechism of the Catholic Church*, nos. 1854-1864.

seriously disruptive of ecclesiastical or moral order to justify the withholding of Holy Communion. Again, extraordinary ministers of Holy Communion are not likely to be in a good position to make these kinds of judgments on their own.

Manifest. The additional requirement that gravely sinful behavior be "manifest" prior to withholding the Eucharist distinguishes canon 915, which operates in the realm of public order, from canon 916, which informs one's personal responsibility to receive the Eucharist worthily. Reception of Holy Communion at Mass is a public action in service to rendering liturgical worship to God; it is not the place for the proclamation of behavior. However sinful, conduct that is not already widely known in the community is not manifest. In something of a parallel to canon 1340, §2 (which prohibits imposing public penances for occult transgressions), and canon 1330 (which prohibits penalties in cases where no one has perceived the offense), the withholding of the Eucharist for little known sins, though they might well be grave, is not permitted under canon law.

Obstinate. As a final protection against arbitrary denial of the Eucharist, canon 915 demands that even those who are in manifest grave sin be in such a state "obstinately," that is, that they remain in their sin notwithstanding genuine efforts to warn them of the spiritual dangers they face and after they have been given a suitable time to repent. In most cases, extraordinary ministers of Holy Communion would not be privy to these kinds of outreach efforts which, assuming they have even taken place, would almost certainly be conducted at a higher level of ecclesiastical administration. This is not to argue that Holy Communion may be withheld only consequent to a direct exchange between ecclesiastical authority and an alleged public sinner, nor that a pre-determined time for repentance must always be given. It is only to argue that, unlike pastors or bishops, extraordinary ministers of Holy Communion are not usually in a position to assess accurately how the requirement of "obstinacy" might have been satisfied in a particular case.

Now, returning to the first two cases proposed above, it is easy to see how the first (that wherein the roommate's sexual behavior is at odds with the demands of Christian chastity) does not justify the withholding of Holy Communion, for the conduct is not "manifest" to the community. The second case (that of the pro-abortion politician) does not justify an extraordinary minister withholding Holy Communion because he or she cannot determine whether the particular politician's stance (which itself might or might not be "sinful") is canonically "obstinate." The third case, however, (that of the obscene tattoo) requires more attention.

Canon 915 is drafted in a way that seems to assume that ministers of Holy Communion will have sufficient time and the information necessary to reach conclusions about administration of the sacrament. But sometimes, life is not so cooperative; sudden, on-the-spot decisions might need to be made regarding one's eligibility to receive Holy Communion. The most likely way this question will present itself is in regard to deportment or dress. For example, a neo-Nazi, in brown shirt with swastika armband, may appear one day in the Communion line; a woman dressed in a way that, according to prevailing social norms, seems intended to provoke sexual arousal in men, may present herself for the Eucharist; activists for causes at odds with Church teaching might wear distinctive garb or accoutrements as a way to imply their right to Holy Communion despite their ecclesially contrarian stances. In each of these cases, it is likely (and indeed, it may even be intended) that a minister of Holy Communion will have little time to reflect on the situation and make an informed decision.

It would be easy, and I think defensible, to fall back on the analysis offered above and conclude that a minister's lack of certitude about, say, a subject's degree of obstinacy justifies the administration of Holy Communion under such circumstances. But a good case can be made for exactly the opposite response as well. How so?

In the cases described, a suddenly-confronted minister has only the information (here, based on dress, but other examples such as offensive speech are not unknown) presented to him or her. Now, in a free society, deportment and dress are determined largely by individual choices; thus, demonstrative or provocative dress may be assumed to be expressive of one's beliefs, and in many cases, the content of those beliefs can be assessed by adult Catholics as being inconsistent with ecclesial good order. Thus, in the few seconds a minister has to evaluate the individual message being sent by dress and demeanor, and recalling that all ministers are responsible for the protection of the Eucharist entrusted to them, the decision to withhold Holy Communion might well be the prudent choice. Applying to this case of the extraordinary minister confronted by a man with an obscene tattoo, I believe that the minister was correct to direct the covering of the tattoo (which had the effect of making the symbol no longer a projection of the individual's current attitudes) and that when such was done, Holy Communion could be licitly administered. Had the would-be recipient refused to cover the obscenity, I think the minister would have been justified in withholding Holy Communion.

Edward N. Peters, J.D., J.C.D.

CANONS 517, §2, 534 AND 953

SATISFACTION OF MASS OBLIGATIONS IN A PARISH WITHOUT A PASTOR

The bishop has entrusted a small parish community to a lay parish life coordinator whose term will begin in three months when the outgoing pastor retires and moves away. The local dean, who is pastor of a neighboring parish, will have "the powers and faculties of a pastor," in accord with canon 517, §2. The bishop and the parish life coordinator hope to find sufficient visiting priests to provide Sunday Mass at least once a month. The parish has about 350 Mass intentions which cannot be satisfied over the course of one year. Does the parish life coordinator or the local dean have the authority to transfer this money and these intentions elsewhere? Must the donors be consulted? May the money be returned to the donors and these obligations cancelled? When a visiting priest is able to celebrate Mass on Sunday, must it be a Mass "for the people"? Or does the dean have the obligation to celebrate the Missa pro populo?

OPINION

The obligation to celebrate a *Missa pro populo* on Sundays and holy days of obligation binds the pastor personally (c. 534, §1). However, this parish will have no pastor, so the obligation will cease as soon as the office of pastor is vacant. Visiting priests have no juridical or moral responsibility to celebrate this Mass for which no offering can be accepted. The dean himself, although he has the powers and faculties of a pastor (c. 517, §2), does not have the obligations of a pastor because he is not the pastor of this parish. Any obligations he would have to fulfill in this parish would come by mandate of the bishop, not by the universal law. Nor could the bishop impose on him the obligation to celebrate a Mass for the people of that parish, as that would be contrary to the *Code of Canon Law*, which only obliges the pastor. An appropriate pastoral solution would be for the dean to include the intention of the people of this parish in the *Missa pro populo* that he celebrates in his own parish. This would be akin to a priest who is pastor of several parishes; he only celebrates one *Missa pro populo* which applies to all the people entrusted to him (c. 534, §2).

Canon 953 says that, "No one is permitted to accept more offerings for Masses to be applied by himself than he can satisfy within a year." Mass obligations may be transferred elsewhere when they cannot be satisfied within the year by the priest who accepted them, "unless the donors have expressly indicated a contrary intention" (c. 954). If the outgoing pastor does not want to satisfy these Mass obligations in his first year of retirement, the dean would have the authority to transfer the Mass offerings since he has the powers and faculties of a pastor in this parish (c. 532); he also may mandate the parish life coordinator to do this. If the Mass offerings had been given by the parishioners with the intention that they be satisfied in their own parish, it would be necessary to consult them before transferring the offerings (cf. c. 1284, §2, 3°).

In my opinion, however, the transfer of the Mass obligations should be the last resort. The first thing to be done is to ask the outgoing pastor whether he wishes to satisfy the Mass offerings, or at least some of them, over the course of the year. Canon law gives to the priest, not the parish, the right to accept a Mass offering (c. 945, §1). If the former pastor is willing to satisfy some or all of these obligations, the donors should be consulted, as they may well have given the offerings in the expectation that the Masses would be celebrated publicly in their own parish.

In consulting the donors of the offerings, it would be good to give them the option of having their Mass intentions satisfied collectively in their own parish over the course of the year by the visiting priests in accord with the 1991 decree of the Congregation for the Clergy, *Mos iugiter*.[1] As required by this decree, the visiting priest would be given the amount of one offering and the remaining funds would go to the purposes established by the ordinary (c. 951, §1). Experience shows that most donors prefer that their intention be applied to a parish Mass at which they are able to participate, even if this means that there are multiple intentions at one Mass.[2]

In subsequent years, it may well be the best solution in this parish for all the monthly Masses to be multi-intentional to allow many more parishioners the opportunity to have Mass applied for their intentions in their own parish where they are able to participate. According to *Mos iugiter*, however, this can only be

[1] Congregation for the Clergy, Decree on Collective Mass Intentions, *Mos iugiter*, February 22, 1991, in *Acta Apostolicae Sedis* 83 (1991) 443-446; English translation in Bishops' Committee on the Liturgy, *Thirty-Five Years of the BCL Newsletter 1965-2000* (Washington, DC: United States Conference of Catholic Bishops, 2004), 1245-1247.

[2] The principal rules of *Mos iugiter* are the following:

1) The donors of the Mass offerings must be informed and agree to combine their offerings with others in a single Mass.

2) The time and place for the celebration of the Mass are to be made public.

3) A priest may not celebrate Masses for collective intentions more than twice a week.

4) If the total amount of the offerings given for a collective intention exceeds the amount of the usual offering, the priest may only keep for himself the amount of the usual offering; the excess is to be given to the ordinary for the purposes he has specified in virtue of canon 951, §1.

done with the consent of the donors. Therefore, when the parishioners give a Mass offering, they should be presented the option of the Mass being applied collectively with other intentions at the monthly parish celebration or being applied for their sole intention at a Mass celebrated elsewhere (perhaps even by the retired pastor).

John M. Huels, J.C.D.

CANON 603, §2

ACCEPTANCE OF RETIRED BISHOP AS HERMIT

Bishop N recently reached 75 years of age and, in accord with canon 401, §1 of the Code of Canon Law, *duly submitted his resignation as bishop of the Diocese of X to the Holy Father, who accepted it. As the weeks and months passed, Bishop N experienced a deep longing for prayer, penance, and solitude. After consulting his spiritual director on several occasions, he has become convinced that the Lord is inviting him to spend the rest of his days in prayer, self-denial, and quiet. Bishop N wonders whether he could become a hermit according to canon 603, §2.*

OPINION

Canon 603, §2 states: "A hermit is recognized by law as one dedicated to God in consecrated life if he or she publicly professes in the hands of the diocesan bishop the three evangelical counsels, confirmed by vow or other sacred bond, and observes a proper program of living under his direction."

That Bishop N, who was never a member of an institute of consecrated life, could spend his final years as a hermit poses no problem; however, for a bishop to live as a hermit according to canon 603, §2 raises a primary question: Whether or not he professes the three evangelical counsels "by vow or other sacred bond," may a bishop publicly profess obedience in the hands of the diocesan bishop?

In his *Summa Theologica*, St. Thomas Aquinas asserted that a bishop could become a religious but that "the Pope alone can dispense from the perpetual vow, by which a man binds himself to the care of his subjects, when he took upon himself the episcopal office."[1] But St. Thomas did not indicate that the obedience that a bishop owes the Pope alone is somehow mitigated should he receive the aforesaid dispensation and become a religious.

Since a religious who is raised to the episcopate "is subject only to the Roman Pontiff by virtue of the vow of obedience" (c. 705), only the Pope could allow Bishop N to profess obedience as a hermit in the hands of the diocesan bishop. Yet this obedience would ultimately be directed to the Holy Father, even though it would be mediated through the diocesan bishop in whose hands Bishop N professes it. Bishop N remains "dependent" on the Pope by virtue of his obedience

[1] St. Thomas Aquinas, *Summa Theologica*, Complete English Edition in Five Volumes, trans. Fathers of the English Dominican Province (Allen, TX: Christian Classics, 1948), II, II*ae*, q. 185, Art. 4, vol. IV, 1959.

to him, while the diocesan bishop would have a certain vigilance in regard to Bishop N as a hermit in his diocese and in whose hands Bishop N has professed the evangelical counsels.

In light of his age, Bishop N could make a private commitment in becoming a hermit without any canonical recognition, informing the diocesan bishop of what he was doing. This arrangement would sidestep any question of amending his status as bishop emeritus of the Diocese of X, or the question of to whom he is professing obedience.

Although the *Code of Canon Law* does not foresee the possibility that a retired bishop could become a hermit according to canon 603, §2, it appears that the Holy Father could allow Bishop N to make his public profession as a hermit in the hands of the diocesan bishop, if the obedience that Bishop N continues to owe the Pope is clearly understood as being directed to the Roman Pontiff, and is mediated through the diocesan bishop.

Rev. Msgr. Charles M. Mangan, J.C.L.

ANOTHER OPINION

With the Roman Pontiff's acceptance of resignation, a diocesan bishop assumes *ipso iure* the title of bishop emeritus of the diocese he served (c. 402, §1). It would be important to know the status of this bishop emeritus prior to his episcopal ordination. Was he a diocesan cleric or a member of a religious or secular institute or a society of apostolic life? This would matter in regard to the evangelical counsels addressed below.

It is wise that the bishop emeritus has consulted a spiritual director regarding his decision. Hopefully, too, he has studied and lived *ad experimentum* this form of consecrated life prior to approaching the diocesan bishop for formal acceptance as a hermit (c. 603, §2). The eremitical lifestyle is a most challenging form of consecrated life, requiring a strict withdrawal from the world, silence, solitude, and assiduous prayer and penance (c. 603, §1). It would seem a radical transition from the very demanding active life he led as a diocesan bishop.

The retired bishop's petition to the diocesan bishop for acceptance as a hermit would seem to pose no problem. He would, in agreement with the diocesan bishop, work out a program of life that includes silence, solitude, prayer and penance, as well as the practice of the evangelical counsels. If he had been a member of a religious institute prior to his episcopal ordination, he remains a religious with the obligation of his public vows (c. 705). With his retirement, he can choose a place of residence even outside the houses of his institute, unless the Apostolic See has provided otherwise (c. 707, §1).

While the *Code of Canon Law* does not address the bishop emeritus who is a member of a society of apostolic life or a secular institute, the same would seem to hold true as for a religious, *mutatis mutandis*. If the bishop emeritus is bound to live the evangelical counsels by public vows, a sacred bond, or some other bond (cc. 607, §2; 712; 731, §2), it would seem he could continue to live the obligations of the evangelical counsels in accord with the eremitical lifestyle. If he is a diocesan cleric, and does not have the prior obligation through the public vows of religious life or another bond to live the evangelical counsels, there would seem to be no difficulty in his publicly professing them in the hands of the diocesan bishop by a vow or other sacred bond (c. 603, §2).

As a cleric, the bishop emeritus is obliged to perfect continence and celibacy (c. 277, §1). Clerics are also obliged to a simple lifestyle, giving the excess of their temporal goods to meet the needs of the Church and to engage in works of charity (c. 282). Since the Code requires that adequate support be provided for a retired bishop (c. 402, §2), there would seem to be no concern on the part of a diocese for the bishop emeritus's not being able to provide for his basic necessities or health care. Clerics are obliged to reverence and obey the Supreme Pontiff and their own ordinary (c. 273). The counsel of obedience would also seem to require that the bishop emeritus remain faithful to the program of life made in agreement with the diocesan bishop. As a hermit, the bishop emeritus would not participate in the more active care of souls in the diocese he once served as pastor; however, his eremitical life of prayer and penance in a fraternal spirit and agreement with the diocesan bishop would prove an invaluable witness to the people of the diocese.[1]

Sr. Rose McDermott, S.S.J., J.C.D.

[1] Congregation for Bishops, *Apostolorum successores*, "Directory for the Pastoral Ministry of Bishops" (Cittá del Vaticano: Libreria Editrice Vaticana, 2004), no. 226.

Canon 702

SISTER LEAVING INSTITUTE FOLLOWING EXCLAUSTRATION

A Vicar for Religious asks for advice about a telephone call received from a major superior of a religious institute. A sister in perpetual vows has been on exclaustration and has decided to leave the institute. The institute is located in the United States. The member is from a third world country and is returning to her home. The superior wants to know if there is some sort of "established standard" regarding what should be done for the sister in this type of situation.

OPINION

While an individual who leaves a religious institute has no right to claim any financial assistance from the institute, canon 702 indicates that the institute should observe equity and gospel charity toward a member who is about to separate. The reason the canon expresses such concepts is based on the fact that a membership relationship, and not an employment relationship, is ending. While one can dedicate oneself totally to God by giving service to others outside of a religious institute, departure means that this act of selfless giving will not take place within this particular institute. It is not the same as someone who is severing employment in a secular profession. In providing such assistance to a departing member, however, the institute should not endanger either its own patrimony or the care of its members. While there is no "established standard" for anyone who leaves a religious institute, there are key concepts which should be kept in mind when providing for the needs of a departing member.

One of the issues is the current state of affairs in this particular institute. You indicated that it is a small one. The median age is 68 years. Apart from minimal Social Security contributions, there is virtually no pension provision since the sisters were engaged in either their own institutions of health care or diocesan-owned schools. Hence, their ability to provide for the retirement needs of their own institute is beginning to present a variety of problems. Furthermore, you indicated that only one woman is in the process of discerning a call to this institute. There are no novices. Two sisters are in temporary vows.

Consideration should also be given to the age of the individual leaving the institute, her health, how many employable years she has left, and her educational background. In speaking with you further, it became clear that the member is 42 years old, enjoys good health, and has a Master's degree in teaching. She obtained this degree while she was in the institute. Throughout her teaching career, she has been known as a model teacher. She hopes to be able to obtain a teaching job in her own country. While she has made some inquiries while on her home visit, nothing has materialized so far. She also realizes that teachers make a poor salary in her own country.

Other factors include any resources that she might have. You said that, while on exclaustration in the United States, she has been living in a furnished apartment and has been leasing a car. Her employer has been providing the usual benefits. She has been able to save about $3,000. Having enjoyed this independence, she hopes to find a place of her own when she returns to her homeland. While in transition she intends to live with her brother and his wife. She has not finalized such plans, but knows that they have a spare bedroom. She indicated that she realizes that the car she has been leasing has to be returned. In order to break the lease, two more car payments have to be made. You also said that when she entered the institute, she had nothing except for the clothes on her back. She does not expect to inherit anything other than a few sentimental objects. A dowry was not required at the time of her entrance into the institute.

Given the situation, it appears that the sister is in good health and is employable for a number of years. While she still needs to finalize her housing situation, she has some idea about where she will live. During this period of transition you might want to recommend to the superior that this sister be given a lump sum when she leaves so that she has enough money to support herself for six months to one year. The money she already has and the current situation of the institute should be taken into consideration when deciding a dollar amount. Given as a one time gift, a lump sum has the advantage of ending the relationship. The sister should also be counseled about the fact that she will probably not be able to enjoy the sort of security that she had while a member of the institute.

Eileen C. Jaramillo, M.Div., J.C.L.

Canon 849

CONSEQUENCES OF INVALID BAPTISM

On February 1, 2008, the Congregation for the Doctrine of the Faith responded to the questions: (1) "Whether the Baptism conferred with the formulas 'I baptize you in the name of the Creator, and of the Redeemer, and of the Sanctifier' and 'I baptize you in the name of the Creator, and of the Liberator, and of the Sustainer' is valid?"; and (2) "Whether the persons baptized with those formulas have to be baptized in forma absoluta*?"*[1] *The responses approved by Pope Benedict XVI are that both forms are invalid and that persons so baptized should be baptized absolutely. What are the consequences of invalid baptism and what should be done to remedy such an unfortunate situation?*[2]

OPINION

One would attempt in vain to invoke the principle *Ecclesia supplet* as a solution to the problems caused by attempting to baptize with an invalid form. This principle is applicable only when it is a question of an individual acting without the necessary faculty to administer the sacrament of penance or confirmation, or of officiating at a marriage when the law supplies the necessary faculty (c. 144). It is not applicable in cases where there is a defect in the essential matter or form of a sacrament. It is certain that God in conferring grace is not limited by the sacraments. Thus, even though baptism is necessary for salvation, the Church teaches that a sincere individual can be saved by baptism of desire (*in voto*). However, baptism of desire does not make it possible for a person to receive the other sacraments validly. The *Code of Canon Law* expresses the necessity of baptism for the reception of the other sacraments by repeating the traditional expression calling it "the gateway to the sacraments" (*ianua sacramentorum*).

[1] Congregation for the Doctrine of the Faith, "'*Responsa ad proposita dubia*' Concerning the Use of Certain Baptismal Formulas with Inclusive Language," in *L'Osservatore Romano*, Weekly Edition in English, (March 5, 2008) 9. Cf. Also, pages 17-18 supra.

[2] For an earlier consideration of this topic see the opinions of John M. Huels and James C. Gurzynski in *CLSA Advisory Opinions 1984-1993*, ed. Patrick J. Cogan, S.A. (Washington, DC: Canon Law Society of America, 1995), 252-255. For a more extensive commentary on the canonical implications of the February 1, 2008, responses, see Urbano Navarrete, "Le conseguenze canoniche e pastorali," in *L'Osservatore Romano* (March 1, 2008) 6.

Sad to say, even some Catholic priests—with the intention of being politically correct or inclusive—have attempted to baptize using such a defective form. However, the presumption is that Catholic priests and deacons, as well as ministers of other Christian communities, employed only the form for baptism found in their approved liturgical books or rituals.

Whenever it is realized that an individual's baptism is invalid, the person should be baptized absolutely, not conditionally. If a person's baptism was invalid, the reception of all the other sacraments was also invalid. So, what should be done?

Since baptism remits all sins committed, the person should not repeat previous confessions. The individual starts out with a clean slate. Confirmation and ordination should be conferred absolutely. In the case of invalid ordination because of the person's invalid baptism, the person needs to be ordained after the valid baptism. Of course, the individual is completely free to request or not request ordination. The person's ordinary is also completely free to either have the person ordained or to refuse ordination. If ordination is refused, the individual is free from all the obligations of the clerical state. Canons 1708-1712 should be followed to declare the invalidity of the ordination.

All the sacraments, except baptism, administered by the invalidly ordained priest are invalid. The same is true if the priest or deacon officiated at the marriage of any individual bound by canonical form. The invalidly ordained "priest" or "deacon" could not be the qualified witness to officiate at a canonical marriage. Here one would in vain invoke *Ecclesia supplet*. This principle applies only if the person were a validly ordained priest or deacon, or a lay person delegated to officiate at marriage (c. 1112, §1).

What about the marriage of an individual who was invalidly baptized? This is more complicated. If the marriage was with a Catholic or Eastern separated Christian, the marriage is invalid because of the impediment of disparity of cult. If the marriage was contracted with an unbaptized person or a baptized Protestant—everything else being equal—the marriage is presumed to be valid.

Rev. William H. Woestman, O.M.I., J.C.D.

CANON 874, §2

RESPONSIBILITIES OF CHRISTIAN WITNESS AT BAPTISM

Can you please explain to me what the Christian witness at baptism, mentioned in canon 874, §2, does? I can find no descriptions of his or her duties or qualifications.

OPINION

The "Christian witness" at baptism, referred to in canon 874, §2, is an ersatz office. It has no duties in the universal law; consequently, there are no qualifications set down for the role.

The term "witness," which in common parlance has become referred to as the "Christian witness" at baptism, first appeared in the 1980 *Schema Codicis Iuris Canonici* (c. 828, §2), perhaps as a gesture of inclusion toward Protestant Christians who, unlike the Eastern Orthodox, were not eligible for service as sponsors at Catholic baptism under the 1967 *Ecumenical Directory* and who, it was foreseen, would not be eligible to serve as sponsors under the revised law.[1]

While the 1993 *Directory for the Application of Principles and Norms on Ecumenism* also sets out no qualifications or duties for this witness (the Directory still does not use the term "Christian witness"), one might discern for the baptized non-Catholic "witness" that some obligation of good Christian example might be implied, in that the witness was likely chosen out of respect for "ties of blood or friendship" (no. 98, a). Common sense suggests that the closer two individuals are, the higher their duty of good example to one another. In any case, as stated above, the so-called "Christian witness" at baptism has no designated role during the *Rite of Baptism* and, unlike parents and sponsors, has no specific on-going responsibilities in law toward the one baptized.

Note that the witness of baptism who is to be summoned in default of a sponsor's attendance at the rite (c. 875) need not be a Christian to serve in that capacity; likewise, the "one witness" whose word could be taken later as proof of baptism (c. 876) need not be a Christian. If, nevertheless, besides the one or two

[1] Edward N. Peters, *Incrementa in Progressu 1983 Codicis Iuris Canonici: A Legislative History of the 1983 Code of Canon Law* (Montréal: Wilson & Lafleur, 2005), 874; Kevin T. Hart, Commentary on Canon 874, in *New Commentary on the Code of Canon Law*, eds. John P. Beal, James A. Coriden, and Thomas J. Green (New York, NY: Paulist Press, 2000), 1063.

sponsors envisioned by the law, a witness (Christian or otherwise) in fact attended the celebration of baptism, his or her name should be recorded per canon 877, §1.[2]

Edward N. Peters, J.D., J.C.D.

[2] Molina Meliá, Commentary on Canon 874, in *Código de Derecho Canónico: Edición bilingüe, fuentes y commentarios de todos los cánones*, 8th ed., ed. Antonio Benlloch Poveda (Valencia, Spain: Edicep, 1994), 406.

Canon 903

PROOF OF SUITABILITY FOR CONCELEBRATING MASS AT CONFERENCE

I am a religious priest in good standing with habitual faculties from my diocese of domicile. I intend to attend a conference, sponsored by a recognized Catholic organization, in the Diocese of X. On the last of the five days of the conference, a concluding Mass will be celebrated and all priests have been asked to concelebrate. As a priest who agreed to concelebrate, I received the following questionnaire from the diocese for my superior to complete prior to my attending the conference and concelebrating the Mass. What is your canonical opinion of this requirement?

Questionnaire

Diocese of X

Purpose for coming to the Diocese:
Dates(s) he will be coming:
Parish to which he is coming (name & address):
Check here if he is coming for a conference ___

Testimonial of Suitability for Priestly Ministry

To Whom It May Concern:

The Reverend__________________is seeking to exercise ministry or give or attend conferences in the Diocese of X. I have carefully reviewed the diocesan or religious order personnel files, and all other records which we maintain, and I have consulted with those who served with him in the work he has been assigned under our authority. Based on these statements listed below:

He is a Priest in good standing with the____________________________
(Diocese/Religious Order)

Please Circle One:

1. Has he ever been suspended or otherwise canonically disciplined?
   Yes No
2. Have any criminal charges ever been brought against him?
   Yes No

3. Has he ever behaved in such a way as to indicate that he might engage in sexual behavior inconsistent with priestly celibacy?
   Yes No
4. Has he ever behaved in such a way as to indicate that he might deal with minors in an inappropriate manner?
   Yes No
5. Has he ever behaved in such a way as to indicate that he may be suffering from alcoholism or other forms of substance abuse?
   Yes No
6. Does he have any mental, emotional, or physical conditions which might adversely affect performance?
   Yes No
7. Has he ever been involved in any incident which might adversely affect his performance as a priest?
   Yes No
8. Is he an American citizen, a legal permanent resident, or does he possess an appropriate current visa?
   Yes No

Based on my inquiries and on my personal knowledge the Reverend ______________ is a man of good moral character and reputation, and is fully qualified to serve in an effective and suitable manner if he should be allowed to minister or give conferences in the Diocese of X.

I hereby grant him permission to seek to exercise priestly ministry in the Diocese of X for a period of ______________ with the understanding that such ministry is temporary and not undertaken for the purpose of seeking incardination in the Diocese of X.

______________________ ______________________

Date Bishop/Provincial/Delegate

OPINION

In summary form, you may ignore the questionnaire and concelebrate the Mass. As a priest in good standing, without any imposed or declared canonical penalties, you have a right, in virtue of ordination, to celebrate the Eucharist publicly. Granted, you may be asked to show evidence of your *bona fides*, that is, a statement that you are indeed a priest, and a priest in good standing, but that is required by the pastor, rector, or whoever is in charge of arranging for the celebration of the Mass at the convention center (see c. 903), and not the diocese itself, or in a general way.

Further, inasmuch as you have been given a habitual grant of the faculty to hear confessions from the local ordinary of your domicile (see cc. 969, §1 and 103), you have the right, granted by the law itself in canon 967, §2, to exercise that faculty everywhere. While the local ordinary can deny such exercise, he can do so only in a particular case, that is, for a specific (named) priest, and for a specific reason. A refusal to complete an unauthorized questionnaire is insufficient reason for denying the exercise of the faculty, inasmuch as that faculty is one given by the universal law. Further, a negative judgment concerning your reputation and your ability to exercise the priesthood could ensue and the diocese might prove liable for any damages that might follow (see c. 128).

If, for some reason—such as your desire to exercise ministry full-time in the Diocese of X—your superior would need to complete this questionnaire, I would caution him from answering certain of the questions, inasmuch as these questions are too general in nature and therefore request information that should remain confidential, insofar as they do not pertain to any specific and/or criminal activity in either the civil or ecclesiastical *fora*. The right to privacy—a natural right—has been enshrined in the *Code of Canon Law* in canon 220; therefore, inasmuch as certain questions violate this natural and ecclesial right, the diocese simply cannot ask such questions; the superior—to avoid violating canon 220 himself—cannot and must not respond to such questions.

For example, question 2 ("Have any criminal charges ever been brought against him?") makes the presumption that charges indicate guilt, which is simply not true. If the charges have been proven, this question merely repeats question 1, pertaining to the ecclesiastical forum. For the civil forum, it is too general: for example, does the question refer to felonies, misdemeanors, or both? As too general, the question is unacceptable: the danger exists of violating canon 220, that is, asking for information that is not relevant to the inquiry at hand.

Question 6 ("Does he have any [...] physical conditions which might adversely affect his performance?") is also too general. Numerous questions immediately arise: What is meant by "physical conditions"? A facial tic that could distract people from prayer? A limp when walking? Is he on prescription medication? Inasmuch as it is not better defined and limited, this question is also unacceptable. Further, what is meant by use of the word "performance"? This does not seem applicable to the exercise of one's priesthood, but rather to participation in theatrics.

Similarly, the terms used in question 7 ("Has he ever been involved in any incident which might adversely affect his performance as a priest?") are problematic because clear definitions or descriptions are lacking. Does the word "incident" refer to a traffic accident, or to a fall? Does the question refer to behavioral problems, either within the compass of "more grave delicts" or not? As too general, the question could once again verge on a violation of canon 220.

In addition, certain of the questions should require evaluation by experts—for example, whether certain behaviors indicate alcohol abuse or mental conditions (question 5).

Finally, question 3 ("Has he ever behaved in such a way as to indicate that he might engage in sexual behavior inconsistent with priestly celibacy?") is simply illogical. On an admittedly superficial level, one could ask, "What sexual behavior is consistent with priestly celibacy?" But more fundamentally, the question ignores the essential distinctions among chastity, continence and celibacy (see c. 277, §1), and reflects a lack of understanding of their precise meaning and application as well as the nature of the obligation.

Fundamentally, the questionnaire does not refer to the external forum; yet, these questions must necessarily pertain to the external forum only, and therefore the superior or bishop is testifying only to public matters of which he has knowledge.

Especially given that you are attending a conference of a Catholic organization, and especially given that the Mass is celebrated in a place that constitutes a closed environment—that is, one not open to the general public—then you do not need to request permission from the diocese to exercise your priesthood; that is a right given to you by the law pursuant to your ordination.

I realize that a diocese must protect itself civilly from liability for the criminal behavior of people affiliated in a variety of ways with the diocese, but such protection should not (cannot) prevent the exercise of ecclesiastical and natural rights. Developing protective measures must include individuals who know the civil law, but also individuals who know canon law; only in this way, given the complex dimensions of the problematic, may a compromise be reached. But this questionnaire—with its too general questions, ignorance of the Code, lack of recognition of the distinction between the external and internal *fora*, and lack of precision concerning canonical terminology—is not the solution, but rather is the cause of further problems.

Rev. Robert J. Kaslyn, S.J., J.C.D.

Canon 914

ADMISSION OF AUTISTIC CHILD TO HOLY COMMUNION

The mother of an autistic child has prepared her son for first Holy Communion. Because the Code of Canon Law *requires that children first make a sacramental confession* (praemissa sacramentali confessione) *before receiving Holy Communion, her pastor has refused to allow the boy to receive the Eucharist, since he is unable to communicate sufficiently with a priest. The mother is most upset. Is the pastor correct?*

OPINION

In order to place this question in its proper context, we should recall that the *Code of Canon Law* requires a lesser disposition for children in danger of death, who can be admitted to Holy Communion "if they can distinguish the body of Christ from ordinary food and receive communion reverently" (c. 913, §2). The concrete application of canon 914 should be very broad in light of the obligation by divine law to receive Holy Communion, for all the baptized who have attained the use of reason. If there is a question as to whether or not a positive law prohibits an action, there is in fact no obligation to observe it. Catholics with disabilities cannot be refused their probable right to receive Holy Communion. In this context, it is good to recall that the Eastern Churches, both Catholic and non-Catholic, give Holy Communion to infants (cf. *CCEO*, c. 710). There seems to be no doubt that the requirements for the reception of Holy Communion of the use of reason, and sacramental confession for persons who are not guilty of mortal sin, are of merely positive ecclesiastical law.

Pope Benedict XVI wrote that "whenever possible, eucharistic communion should be made available to the mentally handicapped, if they are baptized and confirmed: they receive the Eucharist in the faith also of the family or the community that accompanies them."[1] In addition, the United States bishops have stated that

> It is important to note...that the criterion for reception of holy communion is the same for persons with developmental and mental disabilities as for all persons, namely that the person be able to distinguish the Body of Christ from ordinary food, even if this recognition is evidenced through manner, gesture or reverential silence rather than verbally. Pastors are encouraged to consult

[1] Pope Benedict XVI, Apostolic Exhortation, *Sacramentum caritatis*, "The Sacrament of Charity," February 22, 2007 (Washington, DC: United States Conference of Catholic Bishops, 2007), no. 58.

> with parents, those who take the place of parents, diocesan personnel involved with disability issues, psychologists, religious educators and other experts in making their judgment. If it is determined that a parishioner who is disabled is not ready to receive the sacrament, great care is to be taken in explaining the reasons for this decision. Cases of doubt should be resolved in favor of the baptized person to receive the sacrament. The existence of a disability is not considered in and of itself as disqualifying a person from receiving the eucharist.[2]

This same principle is to be applied for giving Holy Communion to a person suffering from dementia, Alzheimer's disease, other illnesses or brain damage from an injury lessening mental capacity, i.e., a doubt should be resolved in favor of the right of the baptized person to receive the sacrament.

Canon 914 affirms that parents have the primary duty to take care that their children, who have reached the use for reason, receive Holy Communion as soon as possible. The pastor's duty is to see that children are properly prepared to receive Holy Communion and to exercise vigilance lest children who have not attained the use of reason, or who are not properly disposed, receive the Eucharist. In the case of an autistic child who cannot communicate with a priest, the pastor should have confidence and trust in the parents, who have prepared the boy for Holy Communion and have affirmed that the child is properly prepared.

Rev. William H. Woestman, O.M.I., J.C.D.

[2] National Conference of Catholic Bishops, *Guidelines for the Celebration of the Sacraments with Persons with Disabilities* (Washington, DC: United States Catholic Conference, Inc.,1995), no. 20.

CANON 1086, §2

EXTENSION OF FACULTY GRANTED TO PASTOR TO PARISH MODERATOR, PAROCHIAL ADMINISTRATOR, OR OTHER PARISH PRIEST

When a diocesan faculty sheet grants to a parish pastor the faculty to grant a dispensation for a Catholic to marry a non-baptized person, is the same faculty granted to a parish moderator (c. 517, §1), parochial administrator (c. 539), or other parish priest?

OPINION

William Woestman, O.M.I. defines a faculty as "the power to exercise ecclesiastical governance in certain cases or to administer the sacraments."[1]

The New Zealand faculty sheet grants the faculty, "If a pastor (*parochus*), to dispense from the impediment of disparity of cult. The proper exercise of this faculty requires that the usual conditions be fulfilled. (c. 1125)"

Attached to the New Zealand faculty sheet are some explanatory notes that state concerning mixed marriages: "This faculty allows a pastor (i.e., a pastor in the canonical sense, which is not the same as all priests in parishes) to grant permission for such mixed marriages." The intent of the explanatory note is to make it clear that faculties granted to pastors are only granted to pastors.

Lists of faculties do not always clearly distinguish between faculties that are granted by law, and faculties that are granted by delegation. Priests can sometimes be confused about what powers the faculty sheet actually grants to them and what they have already received from the universal law by holding an office, such as parish pastor.

For priests appointed as parish administrators, canon 540, §1 states: "A parochial administrator is bound by the same duties and possesses the same rights as a pastor unless the diocesan bishop establishes otherwise." The rights that an administrator enjoys from the law include the functions that are enumerated in canon 530, such as the administration of baptism, assistance at marriages, and the more solemn celebrations of the Eucharist on Sundays. The obligations would include pastoral care, as specified by canon 529, and offering a Mass for the people on Sundays and holy days of obligation (c. 534). An appointment as an administrator is not a long-term appointment. Gordon Read states concerning canon

[1] William H. Woestman, O.M.I., *Canon Law of the Sacraments for Parish Ministry* (Ottawa: Saint Paul University, 2007), 393.

540: "Usually, when a case of this kind occurs, the administrator will be a temporary figure, pending the appointment of a new parish priest [*parochus*] or until the existing priest is able to resume his responsibilities. For this reason, the general principle applied to a diocese applies here too—no innovation while the office is vacant or impeded."[2]

Sometimes priests are appointed to parishes as "co-pastors." In canon law there is no such office as "co-pastor" and canon 526, §2 specifies: "In the same parish there is to be only one pastor or moderator in accord with the norm of can. 517, §1; any contrary custom is reprobated and any contrary privilege whatsoever is revoked." Juan Calvo states concerning canon 526, §2: "Situations contrary to this are reprobated, whether they are based on custom or privilege."[3] Clearly, a so-called "co-pastor" could not validly dispense from the impediment of disparity of cult.

Similarly, when a priest is appointed as "acting parish priest," this is not a canonical title. Effectively, the person is just an administrator. The ability to grant dispensations relates to the canonical office of parish pastor. Therefore, any dispensation is invalid.

The 1983 *Code of Canon Law* includes the office of "moderator" in canon 517, §1, which provides for several priests to be entrusted with the pastoral care of parish(es) *in solidum*, with the moderator directing the joint action. Gordon Read explains that

> The pastoral responsibilities, juridical obligations and rights of a parish priest [*parochus*] belong equally to all members of the team entrusted with parochial care according to canon 517 §1. The sole exception in the Code is that of representing the parish in juridical affairs, which includes implicitly the care of parochial registers. This is reserved to the one appointed as moderator. Any special faculties which are reserved personally to the moderator by the diocesan Bishop, e.g. to grant permission for mixed marriages, do not belong to other members of the team; they share only those faculties given to a parish priest [*parochus*] by law.[4]

[2] Gordon Read, Commentary on Canon 540, in *The Canon Law: Letter & Spirit* (Collegeville, MN: The Liturgical Press, 1995), 301.

[3] Juan Calvo, Commentary on Canon 526, in *Code of Canon Law Annotated,* 2nd ed., eds. Ernest Caparros and Hélène Aubé (Montréal: Wilson & Lafleur Limitée, 2004), 440.

[4] Gordon Read, Commentary on Canon 543, op. cit., 302.

John Renken comments on canon 517 that, "Only one priest may be the moderator (c. 526, §2; see c. 520, §1), and he alone takes possession of the parish (canon 527, §2) ....The moderator alone represents the parish in juridic affairs (c. 543, §2, 3°)."[5] Commenting on the same canon, Antonio Sánchez-Gil states that

> [E]ach priest receives *identical participation* in the entrusted office and can perform the functions that are attributed to a parish priest [*parochus*] (c. 543 §1). Nevertheless, none of them receives, in the words of the lawmakers or in the Code, the name of parish priest [*parochus*], nor does it appear so in the strict sense (see commentary on canon 526)....[A]lthough the moderator certainly holds a particular and predominant position in the group, he is not the 'parish priest' [*parochus*] upon whom the others depend as though they were 'assistants.' As the codifying Commission stated, the moderator, who is *primus inter pares*, (Cf. *Comm.* 14 [1982] 222) directs the joint action and is responsible for it to the bishop. In this sense, it was formerly said that the parochial office *in solidum* has a similar content to that of the office of parish priest [*parochus*], but not identified with it, for the juridical condition of parish priest is not conferred *stricto sensu* to its holders. Neither does it seem that the *coetus* of priests can be considered as parish priest [*parochus*], as one sector of doctrine states.[6]

"Common error does not apply to cases of *special delegation* of a faculty."[7] The law presumes that priests know the law, and the law on faculties promotes good order and protects parochial rights through competent ministers acting for the Church.

If the bishop does not say explicitly that a "priest supervisor or moderator or administrator has all the powers and faculties of a pastor in universal and particular law," then that office holder does not have those powers.

Therefore, when a faculty sheet grants the faculty to pastors the power to dispense from the impediment of disparity of cult, etc., the faculty is only granted to pastors. Other priests, such as administrators, co-pastors, acting parish priests, and moderators do not receive the faculties of a pastor.

Rev. Brendan Daly, J.C.D.

[5] John A. Renken, Commentary on Canon 517, in *New Commentary on the Code of Canon Law*, eds. John P. Beal, James A. Coriden, and Thomas J. Green (New York, NY: Paulist Press, 2000), 683.
[6] Antonio Sánchez-Gil, Commentary on Canon 517, in *Exegetical Commentary on the Code of Canon Law*, eds. Ángel Marzoa, Jorge Miras, and Rafael Rodríguez-Ocaña (Montréal: Wilson & Lafleur, 2004), II/2:1267.
[7] John M. Huels, *Empowerment for Ministry* (New York, NY: Paulist Press, 2003), 60.

Canon 1127, §2

VALIDITY OF DISPENSATION FROM CANONICAL FORM

A Catholic man requested a dispensation from canonical form in order that he might enter marriage with a baptized non-Catholic woman. The man indicated that the wedding would be taking place in the woman's non-Catholic church and before her father, who is the pastor. Many in the woman's family are quite anti-Catholic, and so a Catholic celebration would have caused considerable disharmony and conflict. The local ordinary granted the dispensation. A week before the wedding, the parties asked the minister if he would celebrate the wedding on a pier at a local lake since that was where they first met, and he agreed. Some years later the parties divorced and sought a declaration of nullity. Is the marriage invalid because of an absence of canonical form, or does it enjoy the presumption of validity?

OPINION

In the case presented, a few questions must be settled: what is the essence of canonical form; what specifically is dispensed in a dispensation from canonical form; and what could cause such a dispensation to be invalid?

The law is clear that canonical form consists of the exchange of consent before a person who has the faculty to assist at marriage in that place and before two witnesses (c. 1108, §1). The role of the *assistens* consists of being present, requesting that the parties manifest their consent, and receiving the consent in the name of the Church (c. 1108, §2). The location of the marriage celebration is in no way part of canonical form. This is often confused in chanceries since the request for a dispensation from form is often classified as a request to get married "outside the Church." Such marriages, however, are in no way celebrated "outside the Church," but only outside of *a* church or *an* oratory (cc. 1214, 1223); the celebration of marriage outside of a church or oratory can be permitted by the local ordinary in accord with canon 1118, §§1-2. The tendency to include location among the integral aspects of canonical form leads some to believe that location is for validity, but it is obvious that the law imposes the obligation of location for liceity and not for validity. When a dispensation from canonical form is granted, therefore, what is dispensed is the obligation to exchange consent before a competent Catholic *assistens*.

In some chanceries the practice is to grant this dispensation only if the parties are willing to get married in a religious ceremony, that is, a religious wedding in a non-Catholic church building. If this is one of the criteria used for deciding whether to grant the dispensation, is the fulfillment of this criterion necessary for the validity of the dispensation? As we have shown, a dispensation from canonical form does not include the location of the wedding, since the location is not part of canonical form; in itself, therefore, the non-fulfillment of such a criterion does not cause the dispensation to be invalid. It could only cause the dispensation to be invalid if this were expressly stated in accord with canon 39 (*CCEO*, c. 1516): "Conditions in an administrative act are considered added for validity only when they are expressed by the particles if (*si*), unless (*nisi*), or provided that (*dummodo*)." (The parallel canon in the Eastern Code emphasizes that these particles can be used in the vernacular.) And so, if the dispensing authority wants to insist that the wedding be celebrated in a church building as a condition for the validity of the dispensation (and, therefore, of the marriage), he must make this evident to the beneficiaries of the dispensation.

In the case presented above, the dispensing authority did not insist that the marriage take place in the church mentioned by the petitioner, and so the petitioner could not have known that there was no flexibility regarding the location of the celebration. If the authority wanted to insist that the wedding take place in the church building mentioned by the petitioner, he should have imposed this as a condition; for example, "In virtue of the power given to me by canon 1127, §2, I hereby grant a dispensation from canonical form, *provided that* the wedding is celebrated in the church building mentioned in the petition."

Another approach to the question is to consider whether the dispensation suffers from invalidity due to subreption or obreption. *Subreption* entails a concealment of the truth, which implies a degree of malice on the part of the petitioner (c. 63, §1). In the present case, the decision to conduct the wedding on the pier was a spontaneous change of plans days before the wedding; there was no subreption. *Obreption* entails a statement of falsehood with regard to a motivating cause (c. 63, §2). The motivating cause in the present case was the avoidance of disharmony and conflict in the family; the celebration of the marriage in the church is not a motivating cause but an accidental cause; it was in the mind of the dispensing authority, but it alone would not have moved him to grant the dispensation.[1] The motivating cause was true at the moment of the grant (and ever thereafter), and so the dispensation was valid (c. 63, §3).

[1] On the distinction between a motivating cause and an impelling (or accidental) cause, see Javier Canosa, Commentary on Canon 63, in *Exegetical Commentary on the Code of Canon Law*, eds. Ángel Marzoa, Jorge Miras, and Rafael Rodríguez-Ocaña (Montréal: Wilson & Lafleur, 2004), I:581-582.

A diocesan bishop might wish to be especially insistent on ensuring the religiosity of all marriage celebrations within his jurisdiction and desire to require that all weddings take place in a church for validity. Could he issue a particular law imposing this for the validity of all marriages? Such a law would be invalid, for it would violate the principle of the hierarchy of norms, which requires, in part, that the laws of the diocesan bishop not be contrary to universal laws (c. 135, §2). Most fundamentally, universal law reserves to the supreme authority of the Church the power to establish requirements for the valid celebration of the sacraments (c. 841). This is not in conflict with the application of canon 39 above, since that application concerns an individual marriage and not all marriages; it is not proposing a general policy; in addition, the condition of canon 39 technically pertains to the validity of the dispensation, and only by extension to the validity of the marriage. Universal law also establishes the requirement of location only for liceity (c. 1118); a diocesan bishop's insistence that location contribute to the validity of marriage would be in conflict with this law.

In conclusion, the dispensation from canonical form in this case is valid, and so the marriage enjoys the favor of the law (c. 1060); canonical form was legitimately not observed. In order to declare this marriage null, therefore, it is necessary that the nullity be proven and established with a definitive sentence after conducting an ordinary contentious trial.

William L. Daniel, J.C.L.

Canon 1127, §2

DISPENSATION OF TWO CATHOLICS FROM CANONICAL FORM BY LOCAL ORDINARY

Sally and Roger, baptized Catholic as infants, are now planning to marry. Roger has informed the priest responsible for the marriage preparation that he has been a practicing Lutheran for a long time and does not consider himself a Catholic anymore. There is no notation on Roger's baptismal certificate that he left the Catholic Church by a formal act. According to the March 13, 2006, circular letter of the Pontifical Council for Legislative Texts on the formal act of defection from the Catholic Church, the reception of this act by the competent ecclesiastical authority is necessary for the validity of the act. Sally and Roger would like Roger's minister to witness the exchange of their consent. Who should grant the dispensation from canonical form: (1) The Holy See, because this is the marriage of two Catholics?; or (2) The local ordinary of the Catholic party, because Roger's declaration to the priest that he is Lutheran constitutes the formal reception of his decision to leave the Catholic Church?

OPINION

The 1966 apostolic letter of Pope Paul VI on the dispensing power of bishops, *De episcoporum muneribus*, reserved the dispensation from canonical form to the Holy See.[1] However, in his 1970 *motu proprio*, *Matrimonia mixta*, the pope said that local ordinaries have the right to dispense from canonical form in the case of a mixed marriage, if serious difficulties stand in the way of the observance of the canonical form.[2] In the case of two Catholics, the dispensation remained reserved to the Holy See. In 1972, the Pontifical Commission for the Interpretation of the Decrees of Vatican Council II determined that the local ordinary may grant

[1] Pope Paul VI, Apostolic Letter *motu proprio*, *De episcoporum muneribus*, June 15, 1966, in *Acta Apostolicae Sedis* 58 (1966) 471, no. IX, 17; English translation in *Canon Law Digest* 6:399.
[2] Pope Paul VI, Apostolic Letter *motu proprio*, *Matrimonia mixta*, March 31, 1970, in *Acta Apostolicae Sedis* 62 (1970) 257-263, no. 9; English translation in *Canon Law Digest* 7:716.

this dispensation also in the case of a marriage of two Catholics when one had defected from the Catholic faith and converted to "another non-Catholic confession," be it a Christian or non-Christian religion.[3]

There are two questions that must be answered to arrive at the correct solution to the case of Sally and Roger. Is the authentic interpretation of 1972 still in force today? Is the reception by competent ecclesiastical authority of a formal act of defection from the Catholic Church necessary for the valid grant of a dispensation from canonical form in a marriage between a Catholic and a person who was baptized Catholic but defected from the Catholic faith?

The 1983 *Code of Canon Law* did not repeat the reservation to the Holy See of the dispensation from canonical form for the marriage of two Catholics. This created a doubt whether it was abrogated because the revised Code could be seen as having integrally reordered the discipline on marriage and dispensations (cf. c. 6, §1, 4°), thus allowing the diocesan bishop to dispense from canonical form in the case of two Catholics. The issue was resolved with an authentic interpretation in 1985. The response was in the negative to the following question: "Whether outside the case of urgent danger of death can the diocesan bishop dispense according to canon 87, §1 from the canonical form for the marriage of two Catholics?"[4] The negative reply makes no mention of the exception regarding a marriage involving a Catholic who defected from the faith. This raises the question whether the 1985 authentic interpretation integrally reorders the 1972 exception and abrogates it (cf. c. 20), thereby eliminating the power of the local ordinary to dispense from the canonical form of marriage when one of the two Catholic parties had defected from the Catholic Church.

To answer this question, it will be useful to consider whether the 1985 authentic interpretation was restrictive, explanatory, or declarative. If it were restrictive, it would have changed the law, meaning that the 1983 Code had implicitly allowed the diocesan bishop, in virtue of canon 87, §1, to dispense two Catholics from the canonical form. Lawrence Wrenn says the interpretation was "quasi-

[3] Pontifical Commission for the Interpretation of the Decrees of Vatican Council II, Reply, February 11, 1972, in *Acta Apostolicae Sedis* 64 (1972) 397; English translation in *Canon Law Digest* 7:750. "*D. Utrum ad normam Litterarum Apostolicarum Motu proprio datarum die 31 martii 1970, quae verbis incipiunt Matrimonia mixta, Ordinarius loci possit concedere dispensationem a forma canonica celebrationis matrimonii mixti si unus sit catholicus, alter vero fuit quidem baptizatus in ecclesia catholica, sed deinde a fide deficiens ad aliam confessionem non catholicam conversus sit. R. Affirmative, dummodo graves difficultates formae canonicae servandae obstent.*"

Just as the law of *Matrimonia mixta* applies both to mixed marriages in the strict sense and to disparity of cult marriages, the same must be understood here by the term "non-Catholic confession."

[4] Pontifical Commission for the Authentic Interpretation of the Code of Canon Law, Reply, May 14, 1985, in *Acta Apostolicae Sedis* 77 (1985) 771; English translation in *Canon Law Digest* 11:14.

restrictive." Wrenn means that it was somewhat restrictive in the sense that the Code contains no such reservation of the bishop's dispensing power. However, it was not really restrictive, he argues, because it was never a matter of an objective doubt, since the drafters of the revised Code understood all along that the dispensation was reserved to the Holy See.[5] They saw no reason to include it in the Code, assuming the law would continue in force.[6]

I do not accept Wrenn's category of "quasi-restrictive," nor do I agree that there was no objective doubt but, like him, I too conclude that it is not a restrictive interpretation. Rather, it is an explanatory interpretation, one that explains the meaning of a doubtful law without extending or restricting its meaning. It is not a merely declarative interpretation, which would be the case if there were no doubt of law. There was a true doubt of law, because one could have reasonably concluded that the reservation to the Holy See of this dispensation had been abrogated by the revised Code due to the integral reordering of the former law, and that the drafters of the Code had simply failed to recognize this. Given the position of the drafters of the Code, however, the more probable explanation, without removing all doubt, was that the revised Code did not revoke the 1966 reservation.

The 1985 explanatory reply of the Code Commission did not change the law of the Code but merely clarified that the earlier law remained in force and was not revoked by the Code. The reply implies that the papal reservations of episcopal dispensing power in *De episcoporum muneribus* were not integrally reordered by the Code; those reservations not contrary to the Code remain in force.[7] Effectively, the reply of the Commission in 1985 was simply acknowledging that the reservation to the Holy See of the dispensation from canonical form in the marriage of two Catholics is still in force, even if it was not repeated in the 1983 Code. Explanatory interpretations, like extensive and restrictive interpretations, are not retroactive, so any dispensations from canonical form by the diocesan bishop between the effective dates of the revised Code (November 27, 1983) and the authentic interpretation (November 1, 1985) are to be presumed valid, in keeping with the rule of canon 14 on a doubt of law.

We are now able to determine whether the 1985 authentic interpretation abrogated the 1972 authentic interpretation allowing the local ordinary to dispense

[5] Lawrence G. Wrenn, *Authentic Interpretations on the 1983 Code* (Washington, DC: Canon Law Society of America, 1993), 22.

[6] See Thomas J. Green, "Dispensation from Canonical Form in a Marriage Involving Two Catholics," in *CLSA Advisory Opinions 1994-2000*, ed. Arthur J. Espelage, O.F.M. (Washington, DC: Canon Law Society of America, 2002), 382.

[7] Another reservation still in force but not repeated in the Code is no. IX, 4 on universal laws affecting religious.

from canonical form when one of the two Catholic parties had defected from the Catholic Church. First, it should be noted that the 1985 authentic interpretation does not explicitly address this issue, since the question asked makes no reference to the 1972 exception (the marriage of a Catholic to an "ex-Catholic") but only to the rule (the marriage of two Catholics). Just as an exception does not change the rule, so also the reaffirmation of the rule in 1985 did not revoke the exception made in 1972. The intent of the 1985 authentic interpretation was to explain the existing law, not to restrict it or change it. It implied that the reservation of this dispensation was still in force, even if not repeated in the 1983 Code. It was an affirmation of the *status quo* and did not affect the exception given in the 1972 interpretation. Thus, the 1972 exception remains in force. The local ordinary may dispense from canonical form, in accord with canon 1127, §2, in the case of two Catholics, when one has defected from the Catholic Church and become a member of a non-Catholic confession.

The second question that needs to be addressed is whether a formal act of defection is required for this dispensation to be valid. A Catholic who has defected from the Church by a formal act is exempt from the impediment of disparity of cult, the obligation of canonical form, and the permission required for a mixed marriage (cc. 1086, §1; 1117; 1124). However, the 1972 authentic interpretation referred only to the fact of defection, to someone who was baptized a Catholic but defected from the faith and converted to another non-Catholic confession (*a fide deficiens ad aliam confessionem non catholicam conversus sit*). The requirement that the defection be accomplished by a formal juridic act that is received by the competent ecclesiastical authority is not applicable to the dispensation of canon 1127, §2. It suffices that the defection actually occurred. Consequently, the local ordinary may validly and licitly dispense in this case "if grave difficulties hinder the observance of canonical form" (c. 1127, §2).

Before granting this dispensation, the local ordinary should have proof of the defection. In this case the proof is Roger's external forum admission of the defection. Such proof is not necessary for the validity of the dispensation provided the defection actually occurred. Thus, even if the local ordinary were to grant the dispensation without adequate proof (for example, on hearsay evidence given by Sally), the dispensation would still be valid because the defection had in fact occurred. Canon 1071, §2 must also be observed: "The local ordinary is not to grant permission to assist at the marriage of a person who has notoriously rejected the Catholic faith unless the norms mentioned in can. 1125 [on mixed marriage] have been observed with necessary adaptation."

John M. Huels, J.C.D.

Canon 1248

THE CONCURRENCE OF LITURGICAL DAYS AND THE OBLIGATION OF ASSISTING AT MASS

In 2006, Christmas Day fell on a Monday. Many persons were asking whether or not one Mass attended on Christmas Eve would fulfill the obligation of assisting at Mass on the Fourth Sunday of Advent and the Feast of Christmas. What does canon law require?

OPINION

Canon 1248, §1 of the 1983 *Code of Canon Law* states that the obligation of assisting at Mass is satisfied wherever Mass is celebrated in a Catholic rite, either on the holy day itself or on the evening of the previous day. This is in contrast to canon 1248 of the 1917 *Code of Canon Law*, which stated that on feast days of precept Mass was to be heard, without any reference to the previous evening.

The 1917 Code required Mass to be heard on the actual day (i.e., during the twenty-four hour period). Since Pope Pius XII decreed that an evening Mass is one that does not begin before four o'clock in the afternoon,[1] the current Code requires assistance at Mass during a thirty-two hour period (i.e., on the actual day or during the last eight hours of the previous day).

Therefore, in 2006, one could fulfill the obligation to assist at Mass on the Fourth Sunday of Advent during the thirty-two hour period from 4:00 p.m., Saturday, December 23, until 12:00 a.m., Sunday, December 24 (i.e., midnight between Sunday and Monday). One could fulfill the obligation to assist at Mass on Christmas Day in the thirty-two hour period from 4:00 p.m., Sunday, December 24, until 12:00 a.m., Sunday, December 25 (i.e., midnight between Monday and Tuesday). One could fulfill both obligations between 4:00 p.m. and 12:00 a.m. on Sunday, December 24.

[1] Cf. Pope Pius XII, Apostolic Constitution, *Christus Dominus*, January 6, 1953, no. VI, in *Acta Apostolicae Sedis* 45 (1953) 23; English translation in *Canon Law Digest* 4:275-276; Holy Office, Instruction, January 6, 1953, no. 12, in *Acta Apostolicae Sedis* 45 (1953) 50; English translation in *Canon Law Digest* 4:280.

Whenever a holy day of obligation (e.g., the Solemnity of the Assumption) has fallen on a Sunday, it has never been held that one should assist at two Masses. One Mass is sufficient when two days of obligation coincide. Similarly, should there be an overlapping of the evening of a previous day with another day, one Mass would be sufficient during the overlapping hours.

The obligation may be fulfilled at any Mass, even Mass celebrated in another (i.e., non-Latin) rite. Consequently, one could fulfill one's Christmas Day obligation by assisting at Mass in an Eastern Catholic Church (such as a Ukrainian Catholic Church) where the Mass of December 25 would liturgically be an Advent Mass, as Christmas is celebrated in that Church that year on January 7.

The matter of liturgical texts does not form part of the obligation. Therefore, attendance at any Mass in any place after 4:00 p.m. on a Saturday satisfies the Sunday obligation, even if the liturgical texts are not those of the Sunday or holy day of obligation; for example, assisting at a wedding Mass on Saturday after 4:00 p.m. fulfills the Sunday obligation, just as it does at any wedding Mass celebrated on a Sunday. The obligation would still be fulfilled, even though diocesan policy may require that a Sunday obligation Mass should not begin before a later hour (such as 6:00 p.m. or 7:00 p.m.), or that Masses should not be celebrated outside churches (e.g., in school chapels or other oratories).

Very Reverend Ian B. Waters, J.C.D.

ANOTHER OPINION

This question involves an interpretation of canon 1248, §1, which states: "A person who assists at a Mass celebrated anywhere in a Catholic rite either on the feast day itself or in the evening (*vespere*) of the preceding day satisfies the obligation of participating in the Mass." In an advisory opinion on this question in 1989, John Huels stated that there are two possible ways of interpreting the law: either by arguing that the literal meaning of the law is fulfilled even if a person attended only one Mass on the evening of the Sunday, or by arguing that there are two separate feast days each with a separate obligation, thus requiring the participation at two Masses.[1] He noted that both are reasonable, thus creating a situation of a doubt of law, with the result being that the more restrictive opinion would not be binding and that favors are to be multiplied. However, additional considerations lead to the conclusion that the second interpretation is the correct

[1] John M. Huels, "Double Precept Fulfilled at One Mass," in *CLSA Advisory Opinions 1984—1993*, ed. Patrick J. Cogan, S.A. (Washington, DC: Canon Law Society of America, 1995), 397-399.

one: there are two distinct days of obligation requiring attendance at two different Masses. This opinion interprets the canon in light of the larger liturgical and theological context, certain statements of the Holy See, and the practices of some conferences of bishops.

1. Liturgical and Theological Context

One of the greatest changes in Book IV, Part III, Title II, of the 1983 *Code of Canon Law* concerns the recognition of the importance that Sunday plays within ecclesiastical life.[2] Influenced by the modern liturgical movement, the Second Vatican Council taught that the Lord's Day is the original feast day and that other celebrations, unless they be truly of the greatest importance, shall not have precedence over Sunday, the foundation and kernel of the entire liturgical year (*Sacrosanctum concilium*, no. 106). Thus, Sunday is seen as the primordial feast, the observance of which should not be regarded so much as a law or an obligation, but as a celebration vitally necessary for the faith of the entire Christian community. Theologically, the Sunday Mass obligation is based on the meaning of the Eucharist, that is, on the need of the faith to express itself eucharistically. The experience of the early Church reminds us that the spirit of the Gospel calls for the celebration of the Lord's Day through the Eucharist.[3] Pope John Paul II reflected on the Sunday obligation and noted: "Since the Eucharist is the very heart of Sunday, it is clear why, from the earliest centuries, the Pastors of the Church have not ceased to remind the faithful of *the need to take part in the liturgical assembly*."[4]

Besides its teaching on Sunday, the Second Vatican Council viewed the liturgical year as the time when the Church unfolds the mystery of Christ from the incarnation and nativity to the ascension, to Pentecost and the expectation of the coming of the Lord. Through a recalling of the mysteries of redemption, the riches of the Lord's powers and merits are made present and the faithful lay hold to them and are filled with saving grace (*Sacrosanctum concilium*, no. 102). This teaching on Sunday and the liturgical year is incorporated into the *General Norms*

[2] José A. Abad, "Title II: Sacred Times," in *Exegetical Commentary on the Code of Canon Law*, eds. Ángel Marzoa, Jorge Miras, and Rafael Rodríguez-Ocaña (Montréal: Wilson & Lafleur, 2004), III/2: 1882-1889.

[3] Edward J. Kilmartin, "The Basis of the Sunday Mass Obligation," in *Bread From Heaven*, ed. Paul Bernier (New York, NY: Paulist Press, 1977), 151-161.

[4] Pope John Paul II, Apostolic Letter, *Dies Domini*, "On Keeping the Lord's Day Holy," May 31, 1998 (Cittá del Vaticano: Libreria Editrice Vaticana, 1998), no. 46.

for the Liturgical Year and the Calendar, issued on February 14, 1969: Sunday must be ranked as the first holy day of all; because of its special importance, the Sunday celebration gives way only to solemnities or feasts of the Lord (see nos. 4-5).[5]

Our present question involves two of the most significant feasts in the liturgical year, the solemnity of Christmas and the Fourth Sunday of Advent. The Fourth Sunday of Advent celebrates the proximate preparation for the feast of the Lord's birth, while the solemnity of Christmas celebrates the incarnation, the manifestation of the God-man in the flesh. Both feasts are distinct within the liturgical calendar and these distinct feasts give rise to distinct obligations which must be fulfilled by participating in their distinct liturgical celebrations, thus pointing to the necessity of requiring two Masses to fulfill the two obligations.

2. *Statements of the Holy See*

Immediately after the Second Vatican Council, the Holy See provided the possibility of the anticipated Mass, permitting the fulfillment of the obligation of assisting at Mass on Sunday and holy days not only during the twenty-four hour period of the day but also during the evening before, that is, from four o'clock in the evening onwards.[6] At the same time, the understanding of the phrase "in the evening" was intentionally "general in order to avoid casuist situations and anxieties."[7] The practice of the Roman Curia in responding to questions connected with the anticipated Mass gives rise to a number of principles that might be used to address the question at hand.

The first principle involves the fact that, while emphasizing the importance of Sunday as the Lord's Day, the Holy See permitted the obligation to assist at Mass to be fulfilled by a Mass in the evening of the day before. On June 12 and 16, 1964, the Vatican Radio announced that the faithful could satisfy the Sunday precept of Mass by assisting at Mass at Vespers on Saturday.[8] At the same time,

[5] See *Norms Governing Liturgical Calendars*, Liturgy Documentary Series 6 (Washington, DC: United States Catholic Conference, 1984), 14.

[6] The legislator uses the word "evening" (*vespere*), not "afternoon" (*post meridiem*). In keeping with the proper meaning of the word (cf. c. 17), "evening" should be understood as any time from 4:00 p.m. onward. See Pope Pius XII, Apostolic Constitution, *Christus Dominus*, January 6, 1953, no. VI, in *Acta Apostolicae Sedis* 45 (1953) 14-24; English translation in *Canon Law Digest* 4: 275-276. See also John M. Huels and Thomas Willis, "What Time for Anticipated Masses?," *Emmanuel* 96 (1990) 34-41.

[7] *Communicationes* 15 (1983) 251-253.

[8] Vatican Radio, Announcements, "Fulfillment of Sunday Mass Obligation on Saturday," June 12 and 16, 1964, in *Canon Law Digest* 6:670-672.

the announcements reaffirmed the fact that the discipline relative to the Sunday precept remained unchanged and that Sunday was a day consecrated as the Lord's Day.

The second principle is connected to the fact that the anticipated Masses must use the proper liturgical text of the Sunday or appropriate holy day. After a number of concessions were given to allow anticipated Masses, several requests arose as to the proper liturgical text to be used at these Masses. The Sacred Congregation of Rites responded that it is best to say the Sunday or holy day Mass and to include a homily and the prayer of the faithful.[9] Moreover, in light of the many requests for the faculty to have anticipated Masses, the Congregation requested that, whenever the Congregation of the Council granted to local ordinaries the power to allow the faithful of their dioceses to satisfy the Sunday or holy day precept, that the pertinent rescript would mention that the Sacred Congregation of Rites had mandated that "*the Sunday or holyday liturgical texts are to be used* and that the homily and prayer of the faithful *are not* to be omitted."[10] A few years later these provisions were incorporated in the instruction on eucharistic worship, *Eucharisticum Mysterium*, issued by the Sacred Congregation of Rites on May 25, 1967.[11] The instruction stated that the anticipated Mass for Sundays or holy days may be celebrated only in the evening and that the Mass celebrated was that assigned in the calendar to Sunday, and the homily and the prayer of the faithful were not to be omitted (no. 28).

In light of the provisions of *Eucharisticum Mysterium*, a third principle arose in response to the question regarding whether or not a Catholic satisfies one's Sunday obligation by attending a Nuptial Mass or a funeral on Saturday evening or on the vigil of a holy day of obligation. The Sacred Congregation for the Clergy stated that, while the instructions of *Eucharisticum Mysterium* (no. 28) must be followed, special prayers can be said for the married couple or the dead person during the celebration of the Mass; "In any case, however, a Catholic satisfies his

[9] Sacred Congregation of Rites, Reply, [1965], *Notitiae* 1 (1965) 307, no. 87.

[10] Sacred Congregation of Rites, Letter, *Impetrata prius*, to Cardinal P. Ciriaci, Prefect of the Congregation of the Council, September 25, 1965, in *Notitiae* 2 (1966) 14; English translation in International Commission on English in the Liturgy, *Documents on the Liturgy 1963-1979: Conciliar, Papal, and Curial Texts* (Collegeville, MN: The Liturgical Press, 1982), no. 444. See also Congregation for Divine Worship, Reply, [1984], in *Notitiae* 20 (1984) 603-605, where the Congregation noted that, for feasts and solemnities that occurred in the 1984-1985 liturgical year, the Mass to be celebrated on the previous evening is the Sunday Mass.

[11] Sacred Congregation of Rites, Instruction, *Eucharisticum Mysterium*, May 25, 1967, in *Acta Apostolicae Sedis* 59 (1967) 539-573; English translation in International Commission on English in the Liturgy, *Documents on the Liturgy 1963-1979: Conciliar, Papal, and Curial Texts* (Collegeville, MN: The Liturgical Press, 1982), 395-420.

obligation by attending any Mass celebrated on Saturday evening or the vigil of a Holy Day of Obligation."[12] This broad understanding of the fulfillment of the Mass obligation seems to have been the mindset of those who prepared the 1983 *Code of Canon Law*. While the proposed text for canon 1248 had read that the obligation of Mass attendance is satisfied "anywhere that a Catholic rite is celebrated legitimately," the commission eliminated the word "legitimately" since, the members argued, the cause of illegitimacy rests with the sacred minister, and the faithful should not be punished for the fault of the minister.[13]

In the midst of these clarifications, the issue of the concurrence of Sundays and holy days was addressed. On December 12, 1967, the Sacred Congregation of Rites addressed the fact that, in 1967, the Fourth Sunday of Advent fell on the vigil of Christmas and it declared that the Mass of the vigil was to be said on the Sunday evening.[14] Eventually the Sacred Congregation for Divine Worship provided a principle for dealing with the case when a holy day of obligation falls on a Saturday or a Monday.[15] The question arose because sometimes on the evening of the first day (the Saturday or the Sunday), there is a case of the coincidence of two liturgical days due to the fact that "the observance of Sunday and solemnities begins with the evening of the preceding day" *(General Norms for the Liturgical Year and the Calendar*, no. 3). Interestingly, the Congregation observed that at one celebration, some people might be fulfilling the precept for the actual day, while others might be fulfilling the precept for the following day; no mention is made of people who might be fulfilling both obligations. The Congregation reasoned that, in the case of a Sunday following a holy day or vice versa, the best way to achieve completeness in the observance of the entire liturgical day is to apply to the celebration of an evening Mass what is laid down in the case of evening prayer, namely: "If the same day were to call for celebration of evening prayer of that day's office and evening prayer I of the following day, evening prayer of the day with the higher rank in the Table of Liturgical Days takes precedence; in cases of equal rank, evening prayer of the actual day

[12] Sacred Congregation for the Clergy, Reply, "Any Mass Satisfies Anticipated Sunday/Holyday Obligation," April 3, 1971, in *Canon Law Digest* 10:190.

[13] *Communicationes* 12 (1980) 361.

[14] Sacred Congregation of Rites, Declaration, *Cum Dominica IV Adventus*, December 12, 1967, in *Notitiae* 3 (1967) 428; English translation in International Commission on English in the Liturgy, *Documents on the Liturgy 1963-1979: Conciliar, Papal, and Curial Texts* (Collegeville, MN: The Liturgical Press, 1982), no. 447.

[15] Sacred Congregation for Divine Worship, Note on the Instruction *Eucharisticum Mysterium*, [1974], in *Notitiae* 10 (1974) 222-223; English translation in International Commission on English in the Liturgy, *Documents on the Liturgy 1963-1979: Conciliar, Papal, and Curial Texts* (Collegeville, MN: The Liturgical Press, 1982), no. 448.

takes precedence" (*General Norms for the Liturgical Year and the Calendar*, no. 61). This response was used to address the issue of the concurrence of All Saints Day and All Souls Day in 1975.[16] Meanwhile, the Sacred Congregation for the Clergy highlighted another principle when making its response to the question about satisfying the Sunday Mass on Friday; the Congregation did not want "to separate the canonical discipline (namely, the satisfaction of the precept) from the liturgical sense," so that Sunday would not lose all of its real significance.[17] In these responses are found two important principles that apply directly to our present case, namely, the principle of higher rank in the Liturgical Year, and the principle of the necessity of keeping united both the canonical discipline and the liturgical sense of a particular holy day.

The final principle for a response to the present case emerges when the Holy See was asked specifically about the matter of simultaneous fulfillment of holy day and Sunday obligations by attendance at the evening vigil Mass. The Congregation for the Clergy received the question: "Whether the faithful who attend Mass on Saturday, 15 August, would fulfill the double precept of hearing Mass on Saturday, feast of the Assumption, and Sunday, 16 August"? The Congregation responded in the negative to the above case and to all analogous cases, due to the fact that the "indult by which the faculty is given to fulfill the obligation of attending Mass on the evening of a Saturday or of a feast day of obligation is generally granted in view of rendering easier the fulfillment of such a precept, without prejudice of keeping every Lord's Day holy."[18] This reply has a direct application to the present case. Although it was not an authentic interpretation of the law, being only a private reply, it does indicate the *praxis Curiae*.

3. *Conferences of Bishops*

In addition to the principles emerging from the practice of the Holy See, one other indication involves the decision and practice of some conferences of bishops. Since the Second Vatican Council, Christmas has fallen on a Monday about

[16] Sacred Congregation for the Sacraments and Divine Worship, Reply, "Concurrence of All Saints Day and All Souls Day," October 29, 1975, in *Canon Law Digest* 8:868.

[17] Sacred Congregation for the Clergy, Reply, "Friday Mass Not Allowed as Substitute for Sunday Mass," [1977], in *Canon Law Digest* 8:869.

[18] Congregation for the Clergy, Reply, [undated], in Bishops' Committee on the Liturgy, *Thirty-Five Years of the BCL Newsletter: 1965-2000* (Washington, DC: United States Conference of Catholic Bishops, 2004), 450. For comments on this reply, see Aidan Carr, "Questions Answered," *Homiletic and Pastoral Review* 70 (December 1969) 230-232 and John M. Huels, "Double Precept Fulfilled at One Mass," in *CLSA Advisory Opinions 1984 - 1993*, ed. Patrick J. Cogan, S.A. (Washington, DC: Canon Law Society of America, 1995), 397-398.

once every decade (1967, 1978, 1989, 2006), and the conferences of bishops of both the United States of America and Canada have addressed this at various times. In 1989, the National Conference of Catholic Bishops highlighted the importance of not compromising the celebration of the paschal mystery on Sunday, when Christmas falls on the next day. Thus, people were encouraged to attend Mass on the Fourth Sunday of Advent and on Christmas morning, or on the vigil of the Fourth Sunday and the vigil of Christmas.[19] Likewise, the National Liturgical Office of the Canadian Conference of Catholic Bishops noted, in 1989, that

> Sunday is the original and primary feast day for the Christian people, and the heart of the liturgical year. Christmas, the celebration of the incarnation of the Son of God and of his birth as our Savior, is a distinct feast. For this reason, the two celebrations should be kept distinct. It is therefore recommended that no Sunday Mass be celebrated on Sunday evening, in order to avoid any confusion between the two celebrations. If possible, additional Vigil Masses for Christmas should be avoided, and if necessary, only one anticipated Midnight Mass should be celebrated around 10:00 p.m.[20]

Both conferences of bishops highlight the principle of keeping the celebration of the Fourth Sunday of Advent liturgically separate from the celebration of Christmas, and neither considers the possibility of one Mass fulfilling two obligations.

Moreover, one additional action by the bishops of the United States provides a further indication that two obligations of attending Mass may not be fulfilled on the same day. At its plenary assembly in November 1991, the National Conference of Catholic Bishops decided that whenever January 1, August 15, and November 1 fall on a Saturday or Monday, the precept to attend Mass is abrogated; this decision was confirmed by the Congregation of Bishops on July 4, 1992 (Prot. N. 296/84).[21] This decision makes no reference to abrogating the precept on December 25 and, interestingly, does not consider the possibility of fulfilling the double precept to attend Mass (on Sunday as well as on the solemnity) by using one Mass (in the evening) to fulfill the double obligation. The abrogation

[19] Bishops' Committee on the Liturgy, *Thirty-Five Years of the BCL Newsletter: 1965-2000* (Washington, DC: United States Conference of Catholic Bishops, 2004), 1175-1176.

[20] *National Bulletin on Liturgy*, vol. 21, no. 118 (September 1989) 196.

[21] Bishops' Committee on the Liturgy, *Thirty-Five Years of the BCL Newsletter: 1965-2000* (Washington, DC: United States Conference of Catholic Bishops, 2004), 1327. When the solemnity of All Saints fell on a Monday in 1993, the *BCL Newsletter* noted that the obligation to attend Mass was abrogated, but the "preparation for and celebration of All Saints is still given priority in accordance with its nature as a solemnity in the liturgical calendar" (op. cit., 1343). The same thinking was applied to the solemnity on January 1, 1994 (op. cit., 1353).

of the obligation seems to have been a more appropriate response than using one Mass to fulfill both obligations. This points to the conclusion that the obligations arising from two different holy days need to be fulfilled separately.

Conclusion

The fuller liturgical context of the importance of Sunday and the liturgical year provides a significant framework for considering the present question. The Fourth Sunday of Advent and the Feast of Christmas are two distinct feasts and two obligations arise from them whereby the faithful enter into the moments of redemption connected with each celebration. As well, the various statements from the Holy See provide principles that point to the conclusion that the two obligations of participating at Mass on the Fourth Sunday of Advent and the Feast of Christmas may not be fulfilled by attending one Mass on Christmas Eve. The Holy See has consistently highlighted the importance of Sunday as the Lord's Day even though the fulfillment of the Sunday obligation may be fulfilled on the Saturday evening. When the Fourth Sunday of Advent falls on the vigil of Christmas, the evening of the day with the higher rank in the Table of Liturgical Days takes precedence; in this case the liturgical texts for the Vigil of Christmas have to be used. One exception to this case might involve a parish which is accustomed to having a weekly evening Mass on Sunday. In this case, for instance, a Mass at five o'clock in the evening could be the Mass of the Fourth Sunday of Advent fulfilling the obligation for Sunday. First Vespers of Christmas could be said after the Sunday evening Mass, with the understanding that the Christmas season begins with the Midnight Mass (at whatever time–later than the Advent Mass) on Christmas Eve.

Furthermore, the Holy See has been careful not to separate the canonical discipline (namely, the satisfaction of the obligation) from the liturgical sense; thus, the liturgical celebration for Christmas fulfills the precept associated with Christmas, while the liturgical celebration for the Fourth Sunday of Advent fulfills the obligation arising from that holy day. Finally, the Holy See has specifically responded that one cannot fulfill simultaneously the holy day and Sunday obligations by attendance at an evening vigil Mass. Besides these principles, the practice of two conferences of bishops points to a consistent custom of fulfilling the two obligations by participating in two separate Masses.

Ultimately, in light of the conciliar and post-conciliar understanding of the liturgy, as enshrined in the *General Norms for the Liturgical Year and the Calendar*, statements of the Holy See, and the practices of some conferences of bishops, a more complete answer to this case is that there are two separate feast days, each with a separate obligation, thus requiring the participation at two Masses.

Rev. Brian Dunn, J.C.D.

Canon 1263

PARISH FINANCIAL GOALS

The diocesan bishop is considering announcing a capital fund drive on the occasion of our diocesan centennial. He plans to designate a goal for each parish in the diocese in order to reach an overall goal of $5,000,000. He intends a direct-mail campaign to all Catholics registered in each parish, and gifts (and pledges) will be sent directly to the diocese. Pastors will be informed regularly of the revenue coming from their parishioners. The monies generated will be used for several purposes: the renovation of the Cathedral, the establishment of a pension fund for priests, and tuition assistance for students attending our Catholic high school. Does the law require the bishop to consult any diocesan groups before he would establish the goals for each parish?

OPINION

It seems to be a common practice in several dioceses to have major financial campaigns for purposes such as this diocese intends. Certainly, the diocesan bishop will be wise to seek the advice of others before embarking on such a noble project (e.g., pastors, the presbyteral council, the diocesan pastoral council, etc.).

Whether canon law *requires* consultation with others before the diocesan bishop can set the parish goals depends on whether or not each parish will be required to meet its goal from parish revenue if sufficient income does not come from the free will offerings of parishioners contacted via direct mail by the bishop. In other words, if the diocesan bishop sets a mandatory goal to be reached by each parish, with the requirement that any deficit in its amount not reached from free-will offerings of parishioners must come from parish revenue, the diocesan bishop is imposing an extraordinary tax. The diocese is certainly assisting parishes via the direct mail method in reaching their goals, but a tax is nonetheless imposed on the parishes. Therefore, consultation is required according to the discipline of canon 1263.

Canon 1263 states: “After the diocesan bishop has heard the finance council and the presbyteral council, he has the right to impose a moderate tax for the needs of the diocese upon public juridic persons subject to his governance; this tax is to be proportionate to their income. He is permitted only to impose an extraordinary and moderate exaction upon other physical and juridic persons in case of grave necessity and under the same conditions, without prejudice to particular laws and customs which attribute greater rights to him.” This canon concerns the "ordinary"[1] and "extraordinary" taxes which the diocesan bishop may impose only after he has received the counsel (but not necessarily the consent—see c. 127) of both the diocesan finance council and the presbyteral council. After he has consulted these groups, if he decides to impose the tax, he will issue the appropriate decree.

The right to impose a tax is the right to take possession of what another owns. Canonical authors suggest that not subject to taxation are the stable patrimony of the juridic person (see canon 1291), or offerings given for a certain purpose only (see canons 1267, §3 and 1300). Canon 1291 requires the permission of the competent authority to alienate goods belonging to stable patrimony. Canons 1267, §3 and 1300 require administrators to respect and to protect the intentions of donors, which intentions would likely not include that their donations be subject to a tax. In light of these canons, any tax (ordinary or extraordinary) imposed by the diocesan bishop cannot take a portion of the stable patrimony of juridic persons, nor a portion of any donation made to juridic persons for an intention specified by the donors.[2]

The extraordinary and moderate exaction mentioned in canon 1263 is imposed only "in case of grave necessity." It is not expected that the exaction be for routine expenditures, nor that it be imposed regularly to provide for recurring diocesan needs. It is not to be a permanent tax. At the same time, it does not require a necessity of "an exceptionally serious nature."[3] It is imposed by the diocesan bishop upon physical persons, and public and private juridic persons (*ceteris personis physicis et iuridicis*), in the diocese.

Like the ordinary tax, the extraordinary exaction is to be moderate—i.e., not so great as to so harm those taxed as to deprive them of the means necessary to fulfill their own purposes. It is imposed "under the same conditions" as the ordinary tax—i.e., proportionate to the income of the persons, and following the diocesan bishop's consultations with the diocesan finance council and the presbyteral council. Also, as in the case of the ordinary tax, the diocesan bishop is not required to impose the extraordinary tax on all physical and juridic persons; he

[1] The canon does not actually use the term "ordinary tax," but the term is commonly used to distinguish this tax from the "extraordinary" exaction which canon 1263 does mention.

[2] See Nicholas P. Cafardi, "L'autorità di imporre le tasse da parte del vescovo diocesano secondo quanto previsto dal canone 1263," in *Attuali problemi di interpretazione del Codice di diritto canonico*, ed. Bruno Esposito (Rome: Millenium, 1977), 135-138.

[3] Francis G. Morrisey, O.M.I., Commentary on Canon 1263, in *The Canon Law: Letter & Spirit* (Collegeville, MN: The Liturgical Press, 1995), 713.

may choose to impose it upon some but not upon others. Those persons taxed, however, must be subject to the diocesan bishop. If they were not subject to him, he would have no power to impose the tax.

Canon 1263 mentions that the extraordinary tax is to be imposed with the same restrictions as the ordinary tax "without prejudice to particular laws and customs which attribute greater rights to him." This phrase was added during the 1982 private papal consultation with select canonists after the final text of the proposed legislation was presented to him. A literal reading of this canon indicates that particular laws and customs may permit the diocesan bishop to impose extraordinary taxes without the restrictions otherwise placed upon him. Robert Kealy, however, suggests that the canon does not permit new particular legislation giving bishops greater powers than are permitted in the text itself of the canon, "for to do so would make the restrictions of the canon meaningless. It seems that this exception was introduced particularly with Germany and Austria in mind because, at least in some regions where there is a Church tax collected by the state, the state is acting as an agent for the Church and not in its own name and the particular dioceses have to empower the civil finance ministry to collect a tax. Thus, without this clause in canon 1263, they would be unable to do so."[4]

The canon requires that the "ordinary tax" is to be imposed "for the needs of the diocese." It says that the extraordinary tax is to be for cases of "grave necessity." This may include exceptional diocesan needs (e.g., to renovate the Cathedral, to build a retirement facility for clergy, etc.), or other serious needs (e.g., to provide tuition assistance to students attending the diocesan Catholic secondary school).

Rev. Msgr. John A. Renken, J.C.D.

[4] Robert L. Kealy, "Taxation, Assessments and Extraordinary Collections," in *Church Finance Handbook*, eds. Kevin E. McKenna, Lawrence A. DiNardo, and Joseph W. Pokusa (Washington, DC: Canon Law Society of America, 1999), 85. The placement of the added clause seems to apply only to the extraordinary taxation. It does not relate to the "ordinary" tax in the first part of canon 1263.

Robert T. Kennedy observes that any particular law giving the diocesan bishop greater rights would have to be a supradiocesan law, requiring *recognitio* by the Apostolic See (canons 446, 455). See Robert T. Kennedy, Commentary on Canon 1263, in *New Commentary on the Code of Canon Law*, eds. John P. Beal, James A. Coriden, and Thomas J. Green (New York, NY: Paulist Press, 2000), 1465.

Canon 1350, §1

OBLIGATION TO PROVIDE SUPPORT TO SUSPENDED PRIEST

A priest incardinated in the diocese but suspended from ministry has petitioned the bishop for a monthly stipend and healthcare benefits, citing the bishop's obligation under canon 1350, §1. What is the bishop's obligation to provide support to the suspended priest?

OPINION

Canon 1350, §1 reminds the ordinary that clerics who are subject to an ecclesiastical penalty are still clerics and, therefore, are subject to their proper rights including, as established in canon 281, the right to decent support. The diocesan bishop's obligation to provide this support for all clerics in his diocese is established in canon 384. Since a penalized cleric remains incardinated in his diocese, it follows reasonably that his bishop would bear responsibility for him in this regard, as long as he remains in the clerical state.

The responsibility of the bishop in canon 1350, §1 is to make provision so that the cleric "does not lack those things necessary for his decent support (*honestam sustentationem)*." Providing for the cleric's welfare does not mean necessarily that the bishop must directly provide the funds the priest requires, nor does it mean that the suspended priest has no responsibility for himself. If the cleric is able-bodied and capable of working, the bishop can meet his obligation, at least initially, by providing him with some training for secular employment, or even putting him in contact with some employer who might have need of his services.

If the cleric proves himself to be genuinely unemployable, either for reasons of advanced age, ineptitude at a secular career, or some other reason, the bishop maintains his responsibility for the cleric. If a cleric is unable to work, even if he is suspended, the ordinary should provide for his social welfare in accord with canon 281, §2, particularly since it is unlikely that one incapable of civil employment would be capable of returning to active priestly ministry.

The case of the suspended cleric who refuses to work is different. Ultimately, the diocesan bishop bears responsibility for the cleric's welfare. However, it should be noted that neither the provision "for the necessities of their life," mentioned in canon 281, §1, nor the *honesta sustentatio* of canon 1350, §1, suggest that a suspended cleric refusing to work should be provided with the same salary or benefits as one who is actively engaged in ministry. In fact, canon 281 encourages the ordinary to take into account a cleric's function and circumstances of place and time in determining what constitutes appropriate *sustentatio*. Offering a suspended cleric who refuses to work the sort of sustenance which is truly in accord with his function and condition may well convince him that, for the duration of the suspension, secular employment is far preferable. It is worth noting that the 1917 *Code of Canon Law* urged the bishop to ensure that even deposed clerics deprived of their benefices by a penalty not be reduced to mendicancy (c. 2303, §3); it did not require more support than that.

Should the situation of a suspended cleric requesting support arise in a diocese, it is advisable that the bishop and his canonical advisors review the diocesan particular law related to support and remuneration. If the particular law addresses the issue, those norms should be followed. If it does not, it is advisable that the ordinary take advantage of the opportunity to establish diocesan policy on the subject.

It is not in the best interest of a cleric or a diocese for a suspended cleric to remain suspended indefinitely. When a cleric is suspended, the bishop should concern himself primarily with assisting the cleric in a withdrawal from contumacy, and, if appropriate, a return to ministry. If this is unlikely or inadvisable, voluntary petition for return to the lay state, rather than long-term suspension, may be a wise consideration. Canon 1350, §1 serves as a reminder that for the duration of any suspension, the bishop must be attentive to the welfare of his priests. Nevertheless, priests must also approach the situation of suspension with some sense of personal responsibility.

James-Daniel Flynn, J.C.L.

Canon 1394, §1

DISMISSAL OF A PRIEST FROM THE CLERICAL STATE FOR OFFICIATING AT MARRIAGES ILLEGITIMATELY

A priest in our diocese was automatically dismissed from his religious community because he attempted a civil marriage (c. 694, §1, 2°). Unfortunately, this man is causing harm and scandal among the faithful by unlawfully celebrating Mass, administering the sacraments, and officiating at marriages. Is there a remedy in law to protect the faithful and the good reputation of the Church?

OPINION

In addition to being automatically dismissed from his religious community by attempting a civil marriage, the priest lost by the law itself any ecclesiastical office that he may have held (c. 194, §1, 3°), and incurred *latae sententiae* suspension (c. 1394, §1). Sad to say a number of priests, both religious and members of the secular clergy in the same or similar situation, continue at their own convenience to function unlawfully as priests, and even advertise their illicit services as available to the faithful who cannot licitly approach an authorized priest, e.g., to officiate at a Catholic marriage following a civil divorce. Of course, a Catholic bound by canonical form cannot validly marry with such a priest officiating, since the priest does not have the faculty to assist as the qualified witness at marriage. However, some lay persons may salve their conscience by saying that their marriage was "blessed" by a Catholic priest.

One could request the Holy See to dismiss such a priest from the clerical state. However, the *Code of Canon Law* provides a remedy for the situation in canon 1394, §1. The ordinary could warn the priest to cease celebrating the sacraments and officiating at marriages, declare by an extrajudicial decree the *latae sententiae* suspension already incurred, and impose on the priest appropriate punishments, e.g., prohibiting him from presenting himself as a priest. If the priest does not heed the warning, and continues to give scandal, the ordinary could institute a judicial penal process. Since only the Holy See can dismiss a cleric from the clerical state by administrative process, the dismissal from the clerical state can be imposed as an expiatory penalty only by a tribunal of three judges (c. 1425, §1, 2°, a).

If the priest is found guilty and the tribunal imposes the dismissal from the clerical state, once the time for appeal has elapsed, the tribunal can order the execution of the judgment.

When the judgment is executed, the priest is dismissed from the clerical state and freed from all the obligations of the clerical state except that of clerical celibacy, which can be granted only by the Roman Pontiff (cc. 291-292). In most places, depending upon the civil law of the particular state, such ex-priests would no longer be recognized by the state as being able to officiate at marriages.

Rev. William H. Woestman, O.M.I., J.C.D.

Canon 1627

PROCEDURE FOR HANDLING PLAINTS OF NULLITY PRESENTED BY WAY OF EXCEPTION IN SECOND INSTANCE

I am a new judicial vicar at a small appellate tribunal. Recently, a respondent in one of our marriage nullity cases presented a plaint of nullity, because he believed his right of defense was violated. Our tribunal was only recently established as an appellate tribunal, and there is no record of any such case in our recent past. Are we competent to handle this kind of case, and, if so, what process do we follow?

OPINION

A basic distinction in procedural law is that between an action and an exception. An *action* is a juridic act whereby a person with procedural capacity introduces a claim to the judicial authority of the Church—for example, the presentation of a petition accusing one's marriage of nullity, an appeal, or a petition for a new examination of a case. An *exception* is a claim presented by a party in a case, or by an official functioning in the case (e.g., the promoter of justice), by which an issue incidental to the principal question is being raised. A plaint of nullity against a judicial sentence (*querela nullitatis*) can be initiated by way of action or exception (c. 1621).

In the case presented, the respondent in a marriage nullity case is accusing the first instance sentence of being invalid by way of exception. An initial reading of the text of the law could lead one to the conclusion that the second instance court is incompetent for adjudicating this matter. For canon 1624 reads, in part, "The judge who rendered the sentence deals with the complaint of nullity." The judge who issued the challenged sentence, of course, is the collegiate *turnus* of first instance; one might conclude, therefore, that only the latter *turnus* is competent in this matter. Nevertheless, it emerges that this line in canon 1624 is not a comprehensive determination on the matter.

It has been authoritatively acknowledged that a plaint of nullity can be proposed by way of exception before the appellate tribunal. The appellate tribunal is not absolutely incompetent if the plaint is made "during the course of the appellate proceeding '*per modum exceptionis*,' only '*incidenter*,' that is, when the judge of the higher grade has already acquired competence to hear the case in chief, against which judgment an exception of nullity is lodged. In fact, the established practice in the Roman Rota admits this way of proposing the plaint of nullity at the appellate level."[1]

This analysis came to find explicit normative expression in the January 25, 2005, instruction from the Pontifical Council for Legislative Texts, *Dignitas connubii* (hereafter, *DC*). Article 275 reads, in part: "The judge before whom a cause is pending is to hear a complaint of nullity proposed by way of exception...." The cause of marriage nullity described above by the judicial vicar is currently pending before the appellate tribunal in accord with canon 1682, §2, and so it is clear that it is competent to receive and adjudicate this plaint of nullity. Since a cause of nullity of the sentence is incidental to the principal cause of marriage nullity in second instance, it should also be noted that if either party should find himself aggrieved by the interlocutory decision issued by the appellate tribunal, he enjoys the right to appeal the decision to the Tribunal of the Roman Rota to continue pursuing this plaint of nullity (cf. *DC*, art. 277, §3).

Having established that the appellate tribunal is competent, the manner of proceeding must be clarified. Canon 1627 reads as follows: "Cases concerning a complaint of nullity can be treated according to the norms for the oral contentious process." Why does the legislator use the verb "can" (*tractari possunt*)? Are there other options, and if so what are they? The basic procedure for handling plaints of nullity proposed by way of exception in second instance has potentially four unique components: (1) the constitution of a college; (2) the citation of all juridically interested parties and officials; (3) the determination of the dispositive part of the initial decree; and (4) the determination of the other essential elements of an initial affirmative decree. Let us briefly consider each of these components.

1. Before deciding anything, if he has not already done so, the judicial vicar is to issue a decree constituting a *turnus* of at least three judges which will be entrusted with each decision involved in the adjudication of the exception. (This may have already been done immediately when the tribunal received the principal cause from first instance.) This is partially established by *DC*, art. 277, §2, which requires that plaints of nullity lodged against first instance decisions rendered by a college of judges are to be handled by a college of judges. However, even if the first instance sentence was issued by a sole clerical judge (c. 1425, §4), a college must be constituted. For the whole cause is to be treated collegially in

[1] Antoni Stankiewicz, Commentary on Canon 1624, in *Exegetical Commentary on the Code of Canon Law*, eds. Ángel Marzoa, Jorge Miras, and Rafael Rodríguez-Ocaña (Montréal: Wilson & Lafleur, 2004), IV/2:1558.

second instance (c. 1441); and as an incidental cause it is handled by "the college" (*DC*, art. 222, §1).

2. Once the college has been constituted, it is incumbent upon the *praeses* (cf. c. 1507, §1) to notify the other party and the second instance defender of the bond about the nature and fact of the incidental cause introduced by the respondent, giving them an opportunity to offer objections, initial arguments, or other comments;[2] both parties should be informed of their right to have an advocate. The respondent who lodged the exception should also be notified that the petition has been received, that the defender and the other party have been notified, and that the college will decide whether to admit the cause or not after having heard everyone involved. The norm of law indicates that the college places its first act after "having heard the defender of the bond and the parties" (*DC*, art. 222, §1; c. 1589, §1). Failure to do this causes the initial decree to be invalid (c. 127, §2, 1°).

3. After having received and thoroughly considered all the initial statements of the parties, the defender of the bond, and the promoter of justice (if he is involved), the college is to issue its initial decree. This decree is to decide whether to admit the plaint of nullity or not. The law indicates two grounds for rejection of the plaint: a lack of foundation (i.e., it is an empty or unreasonable argument, or it is manifestly impossible to prove); and a lack of connection with the principal cause (i.e., even if it has basis, it is irrelevant to the cause of the nullity of the marriage) (c. 1589, §1; *DC*, art. 222, §1). If either of these grounds applies, the plaint is to be rejected; this decree is to be motivated for validity (c. 1617).[3] If the plaint seems to have some foundation, and if it is connected to the principal cause, it is to be accepted by decree. The decree is to be made known to all juridically interested parties and officials. This decree is not subject to appeal since it must be decided *expeditissime* (cc. 1589, §1; 1629, 5°).[4]

[2] It is highly recommended that the judge issue an ordinatory decree (c. 1617) calling upon the participation of the promoter of justice, who cannot be the same person as the defender of the bond in the cause (*DC*, art. 57, §2; c. 1436, §1; cf. c. 1431, §1).

[3] Cf. Pio Vito Pinto, *I processi nel Codice di diritto canonico. Commento sistematico al lib. VII* (Cittá del Vaticano: Libreria Editrice Vaticana, Pontificia Università Urbaniana, 1993), 354.

[4] Nevertheless, if the respondent is reasonably aggrieved by an initial decision to reject the plaint at the outset, and if the second instance tribunal confirms the first instance sentence, the respondent can propose a plaint of nullity together with a request for a new proposition of the cause to the Tribunal of the Roman Rota (*DC*, art. 274, §3). For the sake of integrity and persuasion, in the petition to the Rota the respondent should mention the second instance tribunal's rejection of the plaint together with the party's objections to this rejection.

4. If the college accepts the plaint, in the same decree it is to decide three other matters: a) the time of the decision (c. 1589, §2); b) the procedure to be used (c. 1590, §1); and c) the nature of the resolving juridic act (c. 1589, §1). Let us consider each of these separately.

a) Regarding the timing, the question may be resolved before the definitive sentence which resolves the principal cause (the nullity of the marriage), or concomitant with the definitive sentence. In the kind of cause presented above, it seems most reasonable to settle the question immediately, since the appellate tribunal's treatment of the principal cause is irrelevant until it is determined whether the first instance decision is valid or not. This is especially evident in light of canon 1682, §2: after a first instance affirmative decision regarding the nullity of marriage, the sentence and acts are to be sent to the appellate court, which is to decide whether to confirm the sentence immediately or admit it to an ordinary examination. The confirmability of the first instance sentence is a moot point if the sentence itself is invalid; the question of the validity of that juridic act, therefore, should first be resolved.

b) As for the procedure to be used, the law presents three options:

    i) The college can use the oral contentious process (c. 1627), which is recommended if the proofs appear to be easily attainable, especially by the simple, oral deposition of the parties and any witnesses and experts.

    ii) The college could decide to use the ordinary contentious process (cf. *DC*, art. 222, §1: *integra iudicii forma*), which is to be recommended if the matter is especially serious (c. 1590, §1), if the proofs are anticipated to be complex and heavily conflicted, if it is foreseen that a large collection of acts must be compiled for more clarity, or if one of the parties requests it (c. 1656, §1).

    iii) The college may also decide to handle the cause *per memorialia*, that is, by means of a brief, simplified trial in which, for the most part, all the juridically interested parties simply submit briefs and any relevant documents to the college (*DC*, arts. 222, §1; 225).

c) In the event of an ordinary contentious process or an oral contentious process, the concluding juridic act is either an interlocutory sentence or an interlocutory decree (cc. 1589, §1; 1607), depending on the gravity and complexity of the issues involved. If the cause is adjudicated *per memorialia*, an interlocutory decree is to be issued, which must be motivated for validity (see c. 1617). Even if the incidental matter is decided concomitant with the definitive sentence, and therefore inserted into the same document as the definitive sentence, the juridic act is still interlocutory in nature, since it would be resolving a cause that is incidental to the principal cause.

The concluding sentence or decree should be communicated to the parties, the defender of the bond, and the promoter of justice (if he participated in the process), in the manner described in canons 1614-1615 and *DC*, art. 258 (cf. *DC*, art. 262).

To summarize, the following documents are to be in place for the treatment of a plaint of nullity handled by way of exception:

1 – a decree constituting a college of judges;

2 – a letter to the other party, notifying her, explaining the plaint, and inviting any comments;

3 – a letter to the defender of the bond, notifying him and inviting any comments;

4 – the same letter as seen in no. 3 to the promoter of justice (if he is involved);

5 – a letter to the party who presented the exception, informing him that the petition has been received and that the other party and the defender of the bond have been contacted;

6 – a decree establishing a) whether to accept or reject the petition, and if it is accepted; b) when the plaint is to be decided; c) the procedure to be used; and d) the nature of the concluding juridic act;

7 – depending on 6 c), all of the essential ordinatory decrees indicated in the law are to be issued: for an ordinary contentious process, see canons 1517-1586, 1596-1618; for an oral contentious process, see canons 1656-1670;

8 – the interlocutory sentence or interlocutory decree resolving the incidental matter, and the communication of this decision to all the juridically interested parties and officials.

William L. Daniel, J.C.L.

CANONS 1717-1731

RIGHTS OF A PRIEST ACCUSED OF MISCONDUCT WITH AN ADULT

An accusation of sexual misconduct with an adult was made against a diocesan priest. Diocesan officials informed the priest of the accusation, which he vehemently denied, but they refused to identify the accuser because the accuser forbade disclosure of identity. The priest was removed from public ministry, he was placed under the same restrictions as a priest accused of sexual abuse of a minor, his name was publicly disclosed in the secular media as one against whom an accusation had been made, and he was told that unless he completed a comprehensive psychological process he would remain permanently barred from priestly ministry. The priest complied with the therapeutic process successfully, thinking he had no alternative and that recourse would put his life on hold for a long period, perhaps years. He was eventually returned to ministry. To this date, he has no idea who his accuser is, or the specifics of the allegation (each time it was explained, details differed). Were any rights of this priest disregarded? How could this situation be avoided in the future?

OPINION

This situation is sad, indeed, and perhaps is based on a general absence of knowledge about the rights of all the Christian faithful, which are assured by codified ecclesiastical law. Given the current situation stemming from the past handling of those who had sexually abused minors, one sometimes suspects that diocesan officials worry that they will be considered negligent (i.e., it will be said that "they did not do enough") in the face of accusations of clerical misconduct. A thorough knowledge of the rights of the Christian faithful (among whom are also the clergy), and of penal procedures, should give them the proper assurance when they have done all they "can" and "should" do. While detractors may wish that codified law were other than it is, at least they would have reason to respect Church leaders who observe the canonical norms. One recalls the expectation of canon 384 that diocesan bishops (who by reason of c. 392, §1 are obliged to promote common ecclesiastical discipline) must "protect" the rights of their presbyters. Those who collaborate with diocesan bishops in their apostolic task would also wish to recall these two canons.

The scenario outlines numerous violations of rights. Based on the facts presented, it appears as if the priest were equivalently "penalized" (i.e., by public removal from priestly ministry), at least for a period of time, without canonical process, and without ever having the opportunity of self-defense. He knows neither his accuser nor any specific allegation against him. The publication of his name in the secular media may have been intended to surface other accusers, but violated his right to a good name which is assured by canon 220, and which must be carefully safeguarded even in the preliminary investigation before a penal process (c. 1717, §2). Restrictions on clerical ministry, as identified in canon 1722, may be imposed only after an investigation preliminary to a penal process identifies an allegation which at least seems true initially and which the preliminary investigation further seems to substantiate. The *Essential Norms for Diocesan/Eparchial Policies Dealing with Allegations of Sexual Abuse of Minors by Priests or Deacons* are particular law for the United States for those accused of sexual abuse of children and youth; its restrictions are for an allegation of specific and especially heinous activity, and even these restrictions must be imposed according to the norm of canon 1722 (i.e., after the completion of the investigation preliminary to a penal process). Seemingly, the mandated psychological intervention was intended to "prove" that misconduct did not occur (which it cannot do); since the priest was told that if he did not comply with a therapeutic process he would never again serve as a priest, one would question whether he offered "free consent" to the psychological process, something on which the Church has insisted for decades.[1]

While it appears that the priest has now been restored to ministry after having successfully complied with the mandated psychological treatment, one wonders if attempts were made to restore the priest's good name in a proportionate way (i.e., by the release of a statement to the public media informing that no accusation against the priest could be substantiated, and that he is therefore presumed innocent of any misconduct). The priest's mere return to public ministry would not sufficiently eliminate suspicions against him; wonderment would still exist.

It appears that this entire ordeal would have been avoided if diocesan officials had never assured the accuser of anonymity. Every priest has the right, as do others, to know the details of accusations made about him and the source from which the accusations originate. Otherwise, he is not able to defend himself.

An obvious problem surfaces when accusations are made anonymously. Thomas Paprocki reflects, "The person affected by an [accusation] should be provided with all available factors....Anonymous or secret information should not be considered. This is necessary in order to refute false or misleading information."[2]

[1] See Jean-Marie Cardinal Villot, Secretary of State, Circular Letter on Psychological Testing, August 6, 1976, Prot. No. 311157, in William H. Woestman, O.M.I., *Ecclesiastical Sanctions and the Penal Process: A Commentary on the Code of Canon Law*, 2nd ed. (Ottawa: Saint Paul University, 2003), 224-225.

[2] Thomas J. Paprocki, "Rights of Christians in the Local Church: Canon Law Procedures in Light of Civil Law Principles of Administrative Justice," in *Studia Canonica* 24 (1990) 437.

It is helpful to distinguish two kinds of anonymous accusations. One sort is a "tip" whereby information is provided which can be readily verified (e.g., an anonymous accusation says a priest has been diverting parochial funds from their proper purpose; this can easily be verified by an audit of parish finances). The other is an accusation that cannot be verified (e.g., the situation identified here, wherein an accuser refuses self-disclosure; this is equivalently an "anonymous" accusation).[3] It would be prudent for the competent ecclesiastical authority to pursue the former; not to do so may be negligent. It is impossible, however, to pursue the latter. Further, in keeping with the right of one to know accusations made against a person, it would appear appropriate for the competent authority to inform the accused of the details of even an anonymous accusation at an appropriate time (e.g., after an investigation about an accusation which cannot be verified). Indeed, depending on the circumstances, the response of the accused may verify that the accusation is frivolous (e.g., a priest may explain that circumstances indicated by the accusation are incredible) or, to the contrary, the accused may admit the truth of the allegation and the proper remedy could be pursued, not excluding therapeutic assistance and ecclesiastical penalties.

Should someone make an accusation which leads to a canonical penal process, eventually the allegation will need to be repeated *in processu*. The judge will be very careful to ascertain the veracity and good intention of the accuser.[4] There, the statement should be made under an oath to tell "the whole truth and only the truth" (c. 1562). The testimony is to be recorded (c. 1567), and signed by the accuser, notary, and judge (c. 1569, §2), after the witness has heard the testimony and been given the opportunity "to add, suppress, correct, or change it" (c. 1569, §1). If a witness refuses to take the oath, he or she is to be heard nonetheless (c. 1562, §2), and the notary is to make an annotation about the refusal (c. 1568). Obviously, one's refusal to make an allegation under oath will bring into question the veracity of the testimony and favor the cause of the defendant.

[3] The weight to be given to anonymous documents is considered in *Dignitas connubii*, art. 188: "So-called anonymous letters and other anonymous documents of any kind whatsoever, per se cannot be considered even an indication, unless they describe facts which can be verified from other sources, and only to the extent that they can be so verified." See Pontifical Council for Legislative Texts, Instruction, *Dignitas connubii*, "Instruction to be Observed by Diocesan and Interdiocesan Tribunals in Handling Cases of the Nullity of Marriage," Official Latin Text with English Translation, January 25, 2005 (Città del Vaticano: Libreria editrice Vaticana, 2005), 143.

[4] Angelo Urru observes: "In accepting the accusations presented to the Ordinary, there is sometimes a trend to consider them too readily as authentic, and that the accusers are reliable and acting in good faith, whereas this too must be proven." See Angelo G. Urru, O.P., "Considerations on Imposing Penalties in Specific Cases," in *The Penal Process and the Protection of Rights in Canon Law*, ed. Patricia M. Dugan (Montréal: Wilson and Lafleur, Ltée, 2005), 289.

The 1917 *Code of Canon Law* had permitted the ordinary to impose suspension, total or partial, upon a cleric *ex informata conscientia* (cc. 2186-2194). The provision had allowed ordinaries to impose the penalty of suspension upon a cleric in virtue of the ordinary's informed conscience without any judicial process or canonical admonitions. Such an extraordinary remedy could not be applied if the ordinary could proceed according to the norms of law. Before imposing the penalty, the ordinary must have conducted an investigation to gather proofs making him certain that the cleric had committed a grave delict justifying such a penalty. *Suspensio ex informata conscientia* could be used against a (materially or formally) occult delict but never against a notorious delict.[5] At least one of three circumstances must have occurred to punish a public offense *ex informata conscientia*: (1) trustworthy and serious witnesses to the delict exist but are unwilling to provide testimony in a trial, and no other proofs exist; (2) the cleric himself impedes the judicial process; or (3) the judicial process or the passing of the sentence is impeded for reasons arising from adverse civil law or the danger of grave scandal. The ordinary was to decide whether or not to inform the cleric of the cause which led to the suspension; divulgation of the cause for the imposition of the penalty was the ordinary's prudent option. The penalty was to be imposed by a decree indicating: (1) that the suspension is imposed for causes known to the ordinary, i.e., *ex informata conscientia*; (2) that the suspension lasts for a determined time,[6] unless the cleric persists in the delictuous behavior, in which case the suspension affects him as long as its cause continues; and (3) that, if the suspension is given only in part, certain specific acts are forbidden. The cleric could seek recourse

[5] Stanislaus Woywod comments: "Ordinarily the suspension *ex informata conscientia* can be inflicted only for an *occult* offense. Canon 2197 states that an offense is occult, when it is not public. The same Canon explains that an offense is public when it has already been divulged–that is, a knowledge of it has been spread among the public (*vulgus*)–or if the circumstances of the offense are such that it can and must be prudently foreseen that it will easily come to the knowledge of the public. If only a few persons know of the offense, and they are of such a character that there is no danger of their publishing the offense, it is still occult. Now, even if there are only a few persons who have direct knowledge (not from hearsay) of the offense, the offense can be proved against the cleric, and the Ordinary is not to proceed with the suspension *ex informata conscientia*, if he can without grave inconvenience proceed against him by ordinary trial (Cfr. canon 2186). If, however, the few witnesses absolutely refuse to testify in court against the cleric (e.g., because their connection with the offense makes them ashamed to testify, or because they are afraid of the cleric or his friends), the Ordinary can proceed *ex informata conscientia*." See Stanislaus Woywod, *A Practical Commentary on the Code of Canon Law*, rev. Callistus Smith (New York, NY: Joseph F. Wagner, Inc., 1948), II:443.

[6] The 1917 Code had urged the ordinary not to impose this suspension *ex informata conscientia* perpetually; nonetheless, a perpetual imposition would be valid. See Stanislaus Woywod, *A Practical Commentary on the Code of Canon Law*, II:444.

against the suspension, in which case the ordinary was to send to the Apostolic See evidence that a delict had been committed, which could be punished in this extraordinary fashion.

The provision of *suspensio ex informata conscientia* does not exist in the 1983 *Code of Canon Law*,[7] and therefore can no longer be invoked.[8] For a priest to be subject to a penal sanction, as in the scenario presented, he must be informed of the alleged delict and proofs (e.g., the identity of his accuser),[9] and be given the right to defense, either through the judicial process (see c. 1721) or the extrajudicial process (c. 1720). Otherwise, penalties (or their practical equivalent) can be imposed on anyone.

In the scenario presented above, it seems that it would have been helpful if both the diocesan officials and the accused priest received the assistance of canonists with particular expertise in the fundamental rights of the Christian faithful and penal procedures. While the diocesan leaders may have intended to pursue a "pastoral" rather than "penal" process to resolve the challenges posed by the accusation, they would wisely have recalled that the codified law of the Church is itself a pastoral instrument whose ultimate purpose is *salus animarum* (see c. 1752).

Rev. Msgr. John A. Renken, J.C.D.

[7] See Kenneth E. Boccafola, "The Special Penal Norms of the United States and Their Application," in *The Penal Process and the Protection of Rights in Canon Law*, ed. Patricia M. Dugan (Montréal: Wilson and Lafleur Ltée, 2005), 257-285.

Also, John P. Beal remarks, "The suspension *ex informata conscientia* has been abrogated–and we ought to keep reminding our bishops that it no longer exists," in "To Be or Not to Be, That Is the Question: The Rights of the Accused in the Canonical Penal Process," in *CLSA Proceedings* 53 (1991) 95.

[8] That the provision of *suspensio ex informata conscientia* no longer exists is assured by canon 6, §1, 3° which states: "When this Code takes force, the following are abrogated:...any universal or particular penal laws whatsoever issued by the Apostolic See unless they are contained in this Code."

[9] Canon 1598, §1 requires that in the judicial penal process the judge, "under penalty of nullity," allow the accused and his advocate to inspect the acts of the case. It adds, "In cases pertaining to the public good to avoid a most grave danger the judge can decree that a specific act must be shown to no one; the judge is to take care, however that *the right of defense always remains intact* [emphasis added]." The same would apply, *mutatis mutandis*, in the extrajudicial process wherein the ordinary "is to inform the accused of the accusation and the proofs, giving an opportunity for self-defense" (c. 1720, 1°). The question is raised even again: Why would anyone wish to take away from a priest his right to defense by refusing to divulge either the names of his accusers or the alleged accusations?

Canon 295 (*CCEO*); Canons 536-537 (*CIC*)

APPOINTMENT TO PARISH COUNCIL OF MEMBER ASCRIBED TO DIFFERENT CHURCH *SUI IURIS*

We have a number of people in the parish who are ascribed to another Church sui iuris. *May the pastor appoint someone who is not a member of the ritual Church to a parish council?*

OPINION

The realities of immigration, particularly in countries like the United States and Canada, color the relationship between the Latin Catholic Church and the various Eastern Catholic Churches. Within the melting pot or mosaic of North American culture, there has been a great deal of ecclesial cross-pollination, some healthy, some not so healthy. Some immigrants and their descendants who are ascribed to Eastern Catholic Churches associate their Church with "the old country." It is not unheard of by those working in Latin Church parishes to have Eastern Catholic faithful talk about feeling more comfortable in "an American parish" than in a parish of their own Church *sui iuris*. Similarly, some Latin Catholics feel drawn to the aesthetics, spirituality, and traditions of Eastern Catholic Churches without attempting to cultivate an appreciation of their own Church's rich heritage.

Of course, the faithful should be encouraged to participate in the life of their own Church and should be reminded of their obligation to observe their rite (*CCEO*, c. 40, §3). If they believe their spiritual needs are not being met there, they have every right to make their needs known to their pastors (*CCEO*, c. 15, §2; *CIC*, c. 212, §2). Parochial ministers—particularly those who have frequent dealings with members of other Churches *sui iuris*—should familiarize themselves with the traditions and norms of such Churches (*CCEO*, c. 41), and they should avoid at all costs any attempts at inducing a person into abandoning his or her Church of ascription (*CCEO*, c. 31), mindful of the ecclesiastical penalty for doing so (*CCEO*, c. 1465).

Still, there are situations where members of one Church *sui iuris* become regular participants in a parish of another Church *sui iuris*, often for very legitimate reasons. For example, an Eastern Catholic man may be married to a Latin Catholic woman and the couple may decide to have their children ascribed and raised in the Latin Church (*CCEO*, c. 29, §1). The man may attend the parish of his wife and children on a stable basis for the purpose of family unity, though retaining his Eastern ascription. While Catholics retain the right to celebrate the sacraments of Holy Eucharist, penance, and anointing of the sick (presuming proper preparation and disposition) according to the liturgy of any Church *sui iuris* (*CIC*, cc. 923; 991; 1248, §1), they should be encouraged to adhere to the discipline of their own Church.

Since "registering" in a parish is a concept foreign to either Code, it should be noted that such registration does not alter a person's canonical status. That is to say, one's canonical parish is determined by one's domicile and ritual ascription (with the exception of personal parishes and chaplaincies), and is not altered by registering in a parish—either a geographically distant parish, or a parish of another Church *sui iuris*. In the case of someone from a different Church *sui iuris*, as long as there is a proper parish within a reasonable distance, he or she should be discouraged from registering in a parish of a different Church *sui iuris*. At a minimum, he or she should be informed that, regardless of registration, he or she remains a parishioner of the parish of his or her own Church *sui iuris*, and his or her canonical rights and obligations are properly situated and directed toward that parish.

Conceding the fact that, *praeter* or *contra legem* as the case may be, there are indeed people regularly participating in the life of a parish different from their Church of ascription, can the pastor appoint those people to the parish pastoral council or parish finance council? Barring particular law on the matter, it would seem that the law would permit this. The *Code of Canon Law*'s treatment of finance councils (c. 537) is the most detailed of the universal laws on the subject, and states that councilors are to be members of Christ's faithful, selected according to the norms laid down by the diocesan bishop. John Renken states, "The parish pastoral council is composed of those who share in the pastoral care of the parish and others of the Christian faithful. Within these categories particular law may make more specifics."[1] If particular law restricts council membership solely to canonical parishioners, then, obviously, it should be obeyed.

The purposes of the parish finance council and pastoral council should drive the determination of whether this is advisable. As John Faris says, "Institutions such as...pastoral councils (cc. 272-275) in which the laity participate are instituted precisely for the purpose of a fruitful exchange of ideas."[2] As consultative

[1] John A. Renken, "Pastoral Councils: Pastoral Planning and Dialogue Among the People of God," in *The Jurist* 53 (1993) 152.

[2] John D. Faris, *Eastern Catholic Churches: Constitution and Governance* (New York, NY: Saint Maron Publications, 1992), 130.

bodies, it would be salubrious for the pastor to select those who would provide solid advice. Thus, if a Latin Catholic man known for his financial genius regularly attended a Melkite parish with his wife and family, it would seem both wise and opportune for the pastor to invite him onto the parish finance council. Similarly, a Latin Church pastor might notice a Ruthenian woman who comes to church with her husband and participates in the parish's charitable activities and seek to have her input on the pastoral council. The universal law does not preclude him from doing so.

Not everything that is permissible in law is therefore a good idea. Filling a parish finance council entirely with those who are not *de iure* parishioners would be inadvisable, regardless of their fiduciary acumen. A pastor would need to be attuned to the opinions and interests of the flock entrusted to his care. In the interest of fostering closer relations within ritual Churches, it would seem advisable, though not mandated by the universal law, to seek the consent of the person's proper pastor before nominating him or her to a parish council. The pastor should take pains to familiarize himself with his own particular law and inquire about the particular law of the person he wishes to nominate before proceeding.

Consulting with his own bishop, and deanery or chancery official, would also be recommended, lest any amicable relationship between eparchies and dioceses be negatively affected.

Timothy T. Ferguson, J.C.L.

Contributors

Rev. Brendan Daly, J.C.D., is the Principal, Good Shepherd College, Auckland, New Zealand, and Associate Judicial Vicar of the Regional Tribunal of New Zealand.

William L. Daniel, J.C.L., is Vice-Chancellor, Defender of the Bond, and Promoter of Justice in the Diocese of Winona, Minnesota.

Rev. Brian Dunn, J.C.D., is Dean of Studies and Assistant Professor of Systematic Theology and Church Law, St. Peter's Seminary, London, Ontario, Canada and Occasional Lecturer, Faculty of Canon Law, Saint Paul University, Ottawa, Ontario, Canada. On July 16, 2008, he was named by Pope Benedict XVI, Auxiliary Bishop of the Diocese of Sault Sainte Marie in Ontario, Canada" On the page listing contributors.

Timothy T. Ferguson, J.C.L., is a Judge and Assessor for the Tribunal in the Archdiocese of Detroit, Michigan.

James-Daniel Flynn, J.C.L., is Episcopal Liaison for Canonical Affairs and Metropolitan Judge in the Archdiocese of Denver, Colorado.

Chad J. Glendinning, J.C.L., is a Defender of the Bond of the Canadian Appeal Tribunal in Ottawa, Ontario, Canada.

John M. Huels, J.C.D., is on the Faculty of Canon Law at Saint Paul University in Ottawa, Ontario, Canada.

Eileen C. Jaramillo, J.C.L., is a Canonical Consultant and Collegiate Judge in the Diocese of Lansing, Michigan and an Adjunct Faculty Member at Siena Heights University.

Rev. Robert J. Kaslyn, S.J., J.C.D., is Associate Professor in the School of Canon Law at The Catholic University of America in Washington, D.C.

Rev. Msgr. Charles M. Mangan, J.C.L., is on the staff of the Congregation for Institutes of Consecrated Life and Societies of Apostolic Life in Vatican City.

Sr. Rose McDermott, S.S.J., J.C.D., is Interim Dean of the School of Canon Law at The Catholic University of America in Washington, D.C.

Edward N. Peters, J.D., J.C.D., holds the Edward Cardinal Szoka Chair at Sacred Heart Major Seminary in Detroit, Michigan.

Rev. Msgr. John A. Renken, J.C.D., is Professor of Canon Law at Saint Paul University in Ottawa, Ontario, Canada.

Very Rev. Ian B. Waters, J.C.D., is Judicial Vicar, Regional Tribunal of Victoria & Tasmania, and Lecturer in Canon Law at the Catholic Theological College in East Melbourne, Victoria, Australia.

Rev. William H. Woestman, O.M.I., J.C.D., is Associate Episcopal Vicar for Canonical Services in the Archdiocese of Chicago, Illinois.